# The TOEFL Master's Guide:

# Speaking Section

## Precise Test Preparation Methods

## Fast Track Edition

# The TOEFL Master's Guide:
## *Speaking Section Precise Test Preparation Methods - Fast Track Edition*

First Edition: January 2014
Revised: March 30, 2018
Author: William Edward Hearn – "*The TOEFL Master*"
Coauthor: Maria Elizabeth Gonzales-Hearn, Ph.D.
Editor: William Edward Hearn and Robert

*Part of the PraxisGroup International Language Academic Series*

To my wife and children who have given me the time to write this book. To Dr. Robert Niebuhr Ph.D. for encouraging me to complete this book. To my students who have enabled me to test and perfect the techniques that work consistently for all who use them. May you all find continued success in life. —William E. Hearn

All inquiries should be addressed to:
Praxis Group International Language AKADEMEIA, LLC
21248 Velino Lane
Estero, FL 33928
USA
www.pgila.org

Library of Congress Catalog-in-Publication Data
William E. Hearn/Dr. Maria E. Gonzales-Hearn – 1st ed.
1. English Language – Textbooks for foreign speakers. 2. Test of English as a Foreign Language – study guides. 3. English language – Examinations – Study guides. I. Title.
Limits of Liability / Disclaimer of Warranty
TOEFL iBT is a registered trademark of Educational Testing Service (ETS). The material in this text has been created completely by the authors, William E. Hearn and Maria E. Gonzales-Hearn PhD. This material is not endorsed or approved by ETS.
**Credits**: Cover by William Edward Hearn, Maria E. Gonzales PhD. & Robert Niebuhr PhD.

TOEFL and TOEFL iBT are a registered trademarks of Educational Testing Services (ETS) of which this series has been neither reviewed nor endorsed.

## ABOUT THE AUTHORS

**William E. Hearn** has been teaching students from many cultures how to master the TOEFL iBT for the past eight years. Today he has over 12,000 hours of classroom experience and knows every aspect of how to beat the test. he is the TOEFL Master. His proven methods enable students to quickly improve their scores from 68 and below to exceed 87 points (the minimum goal) with many students scoring well over 100. Helping students earn scholarships and grants to the university of their choice through high TOEFL scores is his passion and he continues to teach students in his academy in Florida to this day.

**Maria E. Gonzales-Hearn Ph.D.** holds a BA in Education from Florida International University, an MA in Education from the University of Central Florida, and a Ph.D in Education from Florida State University. Dr. Gonzales has more than twenty years teaching experience in Latin and North America. She has been a professor of Curriculum and Instruction at Florida Gulf Cost University for over ten years. She has recently held professor positions at the Univerisdad Autónoma Gabriel Rene Moreno, as well as Universidad Católica Boliviana "San Pablo," both in Santa Cruz, Bolivia. In addition, she taught English to students at the Santa Cruz International School and owns and directs **Praxis Group International** English Language Akademeia, where she offers TOEFL iBT and SAT courses as well as College Placement for students and Professional Development for Educators. Her research focus is intercultural Curriculum and Instruction with an emphasis on how to foster critical thinking by the integration the sociological and cultural aspects on the teaching and learning processes. In addition to co-authoring two trilingual children's books, she has also supervised more than 20 students with their MA and Doctoral thesis as well as has having been published in scientific journals. She has also been a professor of the Dual Language program at Regis University at Denver, Colorado. She is currently a professor in the College of Education at FGCU in Ft. Myers, Florida.

## ABOUT THE EDITOR

**Robert Niebuhr, Ph.D.** earned his Bachelor of Arts degree in History with a minor in German from the Barrett Honors College at Arizona State University (ASU) while an Arizona State Regent's Scholar. Thereafter, he pursued a MA at ASU, during which he won an NSEP Boren Fellowship for graduate thesis research in Serbia and an IIE Fulbright Fellowship for a year-long immersion in Zagreb, Croatia. Upon completing overseas study at the Sveučilišta u Zagrebu, he obtained another MA in history and a Ph.D. from Boston College. Author of almost a dozen books and academic articles, Niebuhr also taught in the Department of Slavic Languages at Harvard and recently taught English at the Universidad Católica Boliviana "San Pablo" in Santa Cruz, Bolivia. He is currently a professor at Arizona State University as well as director of American Global Academy located in Tempe, AZ.

## FORWARD

If you have ever tried taking the TOEFL iBT you know it isn't all about knowing and understanding how to read, listen, speak or write in English. The TOEFL iBT is a VERY complex and confusing test that over one million students take each year and most do not score high enough to even apply to the university they dream of attending. Many students at this point give up while others seek out help through books or TOEFL courses. However, the classes are often time consuming, expensive and not very effective because they are basically grammar classes. Furthermore, many of the books available on the market contain seven or eight hundred pages of information that you almost need a PhD to understand. Besides, those monstrous books give tips like "read faster", and "understand better". Really?! If you could read that well... you wouldn't need the book, right?

That's where "The TOEFL Master's Guide" comes in. The lessons in this book have been designed for the student who does not understand everything they have read or heard, and yet still wants to get a high score on the test. As you can see, this book is compact. It teaches only what you need to know to earn a high score on the TOEFL iBT. These are the exact same methods that I am teaching in my academy now that work for everyone, and all of my students have either graduated from are attending a university now, or are taking classes to prepare to take the TOEFL and go to university in the next six months. Learn the methods in this book, and with only 20 hours of practice you too will be prepared to earn a high score on your TOEFL Speaking section as well.

**Testimonials from TOEFL Master students:**

*"The TOEFL Master methods were really weird at first because they are so different from the way I normally did things, but as I began to use them consistently my TOEFL scores went up. I also started doing better in school because the methods worked on my homework assignments as well. I scored a 98 on my TOEFL iBT"* -Marcello Navajas - Santa Cruz, Bolivia

*"I wouldn't pass the TOEFL test without this course ( simple as this): The PRAXIS course was essential to me. The course provided me the best tips to work with all the sections( writing, reading,listening and speaking) of the test. Also, the course taught me how to read well quickly ( get the basic idea and answer so you don't loose time). Moreover, thanks to the PRAXIS TOEFL course, I was able to get the key words of long texts and answer correctly the questions on the Reading Section.*

*Most importantly, before the course my main weakness was speaking without rambling and going straight to the point. Without the course, I wouldn't get a high score on this section.*

*With respect to the writing and listening, the same thing holds true*
*Now, imagine all of the things I talked about bundled in one single book... I don't think how it could be better!"* - Hugo Vaca Pereira Rocha - January 13, 2014

*"I got a 100, and definitely would not have done it without Bill and Lizzie's help. All the exercises and practice tests and conversations that you go over in the course help you tackle the TOEFL without a problem and feeling prepared. I would recommend this to anyone."* - Carlos E . Kempff Seleme - January 11, 2014

## HISTORY OF THE "TOEFL MASTER'S GUIDE"

While living in Bolivia in 2006, a student asked if I could help them pass the TOEFL iBT. Before I could teach it I first had to master it for myself. After a search of nearly every published book and visiting dozens of web sites, I realized that there was very little clear information available that helped me to take the test and earn a high score. I found books containing practice tests with no help in how to take them and others with few practice tests and lots of information about grammar, but they were huge, very confusing and knowing English grammar was of no help at all. After studying all the books and web sites available, I found myself more confused than ever.

That's when I put my own reasoning abilities to work. I realized that the test is designed using a very specific structure and based on a strict set of rules. By knowing the structure, rules, and procedures used to design the test, students can master answering all the questions quickly and accurately. After four years of testing these TOEFL Master techniques on hundreds of students with excellent results, I have finally compiled all of the information I teach in my classes into one book and now I've broken that into the four sections to make mastering the TOEFL iBT even easier.

## The TOEFL Master Speaking Section methods focus on:

1. Understanding the basic structures of the reading and listening passages.

2. Knowing what question will be asked for each passage type.

3. Listening for specific phrases that indicate information that will answer the questions.

4. Taking simplified notes that will answer the questions.

5. Structuring your responses according to the response rules.

6. Timing your responses to answer in the time allowed.

7. Controlling your accent to pronounce words and phrases clearly.

At present, all of my students are either in a university in the United States, are just about to start, or are just graduating with their master's degree. From my experience in teaching for over 12,000 hours, I can assure you that, if you follow the techniques taught in this book and practice them sufficiently, you will receive a high score on your TOEFL iBT and be ready to enter the university or college of your choice.

# INTRODUCTION

Officially, the TOEFL iBT is said to test a student's ability to speak according to norms in an academic setting such as a classroom or university office and in conversations with fellow students. However, although the TOEFL iBT does test these things, what the TOEFL iBT actually tests is how well you know the structures and rules that the TOEFL iBT is based on. The TOEFL iBT is based on special structures and rules used to determine your score. Knowing these structures and rules will help you to achieve a higher score. Therefore, the TOEFL Master Program was designed specifically to teach you the structures and rules used and how to pass this very confusing and complicated test.

You must understand that the TOEFL iBT is NOT like the tests you have taken in school. The TOEFL Master Program is designed to help you take this very confusing and complicated test in a specific way to answer the questions on the test quickly and accurately. It is important that you follow the methods and structures of responding as taught in this book.

It is also important to understand that passing the TOEFL iBT is simply the first step in being accepted to a major college or university. Once you are accepted, you will have to maintain good grades: especially if you are there on a scholarship. Knowing this, one of the TOEFL Master's main goals is to teach you the study skills that will enable you to read and understand any and all materials that you will encounter while studying at a college or university in the United States or other English-speaking country. These study skills will not only help you to achieve a higher score on the TOEFL iBT, they will ultimately help you to achieve higher grades on all assignments you will turn in and exams that you will take in the university. As with any skill, devotion and practice is required to master these skills and to use them with consistent proficiency. Pay close attention to each lesson and practice each skill until you have a high level of accuracy on your practice tests.

The methods in this book may seem strange at first. In fact, the hardest thing a student has to do is to trust in and follow the procedures. However, once you switch to strictly following the methods and procedures explained in this book, your score will quickly and dramatically rise.

You will also notice that the lessons in this book are concise and to the point. The TOEFL Master does not believe it is necessary to burden a student with extra words when a lesson may be simplified. Should you require a more detailed instruction, please feel free to e-mail me "The TOEFL Master" at william@pgila.org

Finally, this book teaches effective methods and, although it does use sample questions and tests to demonstrate how to use those techniques, it does not provide actual TOEFL tests. The TOEFL Master **strongly** suggests that you also purchase the newest version of the Official ETS TOEFL Guide that comes with a CD containing genuine TOEFL iBT exams for practice.

**TABLE OF CONTENTS**

# Part I: TOEFL iBT Basics

## Chapter 1 – TOEFL iBT OVERVIEW

Description of TOEFL iBT
Structure
Registration
Preparation
The Night Before/Test Day

## Chapter 2 – PSYCHOLOGY

Taking the TOEFL iBT is EASY.
Why take the TOEFL iBT?

## Chapter 3 - SPEAKING SECTION OVERVIEW

Brief description of lessons covered.

## Chapter 4 – BRIDGING THE GAP

Defining what is most important to you.

## Chapter 5 – PATH TO SUCCESS

Definition of Success
Perception
Two Minds
Self Talk
Stay Focused
Discipline
Staying Prepared
Devotion
Respect
Overcoming Fear/Test Anxiety
The Value of Work
Higher Education
Motivation/Incentive
The Power of Writing Things Down

# Part II: Speaking Section Made Easy

## Chapter 6 – SPEAKING SECTION
Overview/Description
Rubrics (Rules)
Nothing to Fear
Dealing with an Accent
Controlling your Speech
Question Types
Independent Questions
Integrated: Reading/Listening
Integrated: Listening Only
Taking Relevant Notes

# Part III - Resources

## Chapter 7 – BASIC GRAMMAR
Basic Sentence Structures
Verb Usage (Tenses & Conjugations)
Transition Words and Phrases
Subject/Verb Agreement

## Chapter 8 – FREQUENTLY ASKED QUESTIONS

# Part I: TOEFL iBT Basics

## Chapter 1 – TOEFL iBT Overview
TOEFL iBT – TEST OF ENGLISH AS A FOREIGN LANGUAGE Internet Based Test

### WHAT IS THE TOEFL IBT?
The TOEFL iBT is a computer-based test that is delivered to testing centers via the Internet. The test is administered by Education Testing Services (ETS), the same organization that administers other standardized tests.

The TOEFL iBT is different from a paper-based test in that you cannot mark the test for later reference or skip to different sections during the test. In other words, you cannot skip parts of the Reading Section, complete the Listening Section and then return to the Reading Section to finish. You ARE allowed to skip questions within the Reading Section ONLY but the TOEFL Master advises against skipping and returning to questions. Each of the other sections present material in a particular order you must answer in order to move forward.

The audio portions of the test are also computer-based. You will be required to speak into a recording device for the Speaking Section so practice recording yourself. You might be surprised at how embarrassed or nervous you can be when you are being recorded. Even if you are comfortable with speaking in front of others and speak English well, many people freeze when they hear the "beep" of the recorder. I have had students who just start laughing and others who don't say anything. The common thing is that with practice all of them scored over 24 on the speaking section once they practiced, and you will too.

In fact, the best way to achieve the highest score on the TOEFL iBT is to practice, practice, and practice. The TOEFL is a demonstration of skill, and like any skill, the more you practice the better you will do. As you practice, you will find that you have strengths and weaknesses. Do not be discouraged by wrong answers. Simply use this tutorial to learn why you missed them and develop that skill to get it right on the test.

It is vital that you know HOW to take the TOEFL test. Although it is good to know English, it is best to know how to take the test.

The TOEFL iBT is a standardized, multiple-choice test, and the good thing is that for the Reading Section all of the answers are on the screen. You have a one in four chance of guessing if you do not know. However, there are also many wrong choices that seem right. This book teaches you how to find the clue in the passage that answers each question and the rules for eliminating wrong choices (POE). By recognizing wrong choices and eliminating them first you will increase your chance at getting a higher score.

## THE STRUCTURE OF THE SPEAKING SECTION

The Speaking section consists of six speaking tasks that require listening and reading. You will be required to speak for either 45 or 60 seconds depending on the task, and you have 20 minutes to complete the entire section. To earn a high score, you must take and use notes in this section. Questions 1 and 2 allow for only 15 seconds of preparation time, Questions 3 and 4 allow for 30 seconds of preparation and Questions 5 and 6 give you 20 seconds to prepare your answer. You will speak for a total of approximately 5 minutes and 30 seconds over all to answer all six questions.

## HOW IS THE SPEAKING SECTION of the TOEFL iBT SCORED?

Your speech will be scored on how well you followed the structures and rules(rubric) set by ETS. The rubric is explained in chapter 6. The short answer is that you will receive a score from 0 to 30 in this section. The average score for the Speaking section of students in non-European countries is 21. That is why the TOEFL Master's methods are designed to help you score a *minimum* of 24. The minimum goal for your score should be 24 points and do your best to exceed 27 points. This is possible by following the methods taught in this book.

## HOW ARE THE SCORES USED?

Colleges and universities will use your TOEFL iBT scores when considering your application. In fact, most colleges and universities that require a TOEFL score will not even accept an application without it. The TOEFL Master strongly suggests that, before deciding on a college or university, check the TOEFL score requirements to see what minimum score you must achieve in order to apply, then work diligently to surpass that score by a minimum of 10 points. For example, if the university you wish to apply to requires a minimum score of 80, you should do your best to score a minimum of 90 on your TOEFL iBT. Keep in mind that getting a high score on your TOEFL iBT does not guarantee you admittance into a particular college or university, but getting a low score will definitely prevent you from even being able to apply.

## REGISTERING FOR THE TOEFL IBT ONLINE

The easiest way to register for the TOEFL iBT is online at:

# www.ets.org/toefl/index.html

Be sure to have your official I.D. and passport ready to fill in the registration forms. Take your time and be careful to enter the information correctly. You MUST fill in the information EXACTLY as it is on your I.D. **Any discrepancies in information such as the spelling of your name, address and phone number, and document number may likely cause you to be rejected at the testing center.** Furthermore, once you have completed your registration, you will be given an ETS ID number. NEVER LOSE THAT NUMBER!!!!!

COPY AND PASTE YOUR ETS ID # ALONG WITH YOUR USER NAME AND PASSWORD AND E-MAIL IT TO YOURSELF FOR FUTURE REFERENCE.

You CANNOT create a new account!! EVER!!!!! If you don't remember your password, you will need your ETS ID to access your account. I stress this because it is very difficult to access your account if you forget your information, and it is VERY difficult to make changes if you get it wrong the first time.

NOTE: If you have moved and live at a different address than the one printed on your I.D. **make sure you enter the address that is on your I.D. that you put on your TOEFL registration!**

The TOEFL Master highly recommends that you take the practice tests on the Official TOEFL website:   http://toeflpractice.ets.org

## BE PREPARED

1. **Know the Directions**: Learn the directions ahead of time so you do not waste time reading them during the test. Specifically, keep in mind the methods and procedures that you learn and practice from this book. The official directions instruct a different approach to taking the test. However, **the TOEFL Master methods are designed to specifically help you answer questions quickly and accurately**.

2. **Have a Plan**: Practice using the procedures for answering the Reading questions as described and taught in this book. Just knowing how to do something isn't enough Practice is the key to a high score. The TOEFL Master **strongly** suggests you purchase the "Official TOEFL iBT Tests with Audio(McGraw Hill's TOEFL iBT) by Educational Testing Service" available on Amazon.com and take ALL of the Reading practice tests until you can use the methods naturally without thinking about them.

3. **Know the Sections**: The four sections are Reading, Listening, Speaking, and Writing: in that order. Know the format and the question types used in the test for each one.

4. **Practice Strategies**:
    A. Most people believe that they must study many different subjects in order to prepare for the TOEFL iBT. This simply is not true. ALL of the information needed to answer the questions on the TOEFL iBT Reading Section is provided on the test. In fact, if you use information that is not presented on the test, you will answer the questions incorrectly. Rather than study many subjects unnecessarily, learn the structures that the passages are based on, the rules, the methods and the procedures for answering questions taught in this book and practice until you use them without thinking about it. Practice them for a minimum of 1 hour a day (Three 20 minute tests). The TOEFL Master strongly suggests 10-15 hours of practice in each section before attempting to take the actual TOEFL iBT to achieve your maximum score.

B. Process of Elimination (POE) is the most important tool for getting a high score on the TOEFL iBT. Learn it; use it in all sections to answer questions.

5. **Go over your Practice Tests**: Review question types that were difficult for you and understand why you missed them. Review your structures and procedures for answering the question types that are difficult for you and practice them until you can master them.

## THE DAY BEFORE TEST DAY

Cramming, or intense studying immediately prior to an event like the TOEFL iBT simply does not work. So, if you have been practicing regularly for the past weeks and really know how to use the processes and procedures taught in this book, you are as good as you can be the day before the test, so relax! This is a day to simply watch TV in English, listen to music and songs in English, or read a good book written in English. These things will keep your mind in the "English" mode of thought, and that will help you tremendously on test day.

Furthermore, a rested body and mind is needed to take the 3 hour 45 minute to 4 hour 30 minutes long TOEFL iBT. Therefore, the TOEFL Master strongly recommends that you get to sleep no later than 11 PM the night before taking the test. Sleep well knowing that you will pass your test and are on your way to a bright and successful future.

## TEST DAY

1. Wake early on test day. You should be awake and getting ready to leave for the testing center at least two hours before test taking time.

2. Your mind needs nutrients to work, so have a good breakfast. If you can, have fresh fruit/juice, milk and cereal, and/or eggs.

3. **AVOID ENERGY DRINKS**!!! Energy drinks make you nervous and make it harder to concentrate.

4. Take a short walk before taking the TOEFL iBT. Research has proven that walking before taking a test improves test scores. Walking increases circulation and blood flow to the brain giving it the vital nutrients it needs to think effectively.

5. Do a little reading as well as speaking and listening in English to get your brain in the "English" mode.

6. Getting to the testing center early also helps you to relax and to feel prepared, so get to the testing site 15 - 30 minutes early. This way you will not feel rushed through the test.

7. Be sure to have your official photo identification and registration letter from ETS. Without these two documents you will not be permitted to take the test.

8. **DO NOT TAKE** food, drinks, briefcase, backpack, laptop computer, or anything else to the testing center. The testing center will provide you with pencils and paper for taking notes. Nothing else is needed.

9. **TURN OFF YOUR CELL PHONE.** Distractions during the test are bad. Having someone think that you are cheating and cancel your test is worse. Don't give anyone the chance to think that you might be cheating. Following test center rules is vital to your success.

# Chapter 2 – THE PSYCHOLOGY OF THE TOEFL iBT
Taking the TOEFL iBT is EASY!

Most of my students once believed that the TOEFL iBT must be a very complicated test because it is so important. Of course . . . it is important. In fact, if a student doesn't earn a certain minimum score, they won't even qualify to apply to a university or college. In fact, nearly 1,000,000 students worldwide take the TOEFL iBT each year earning an average score of 68 out of 120. While most colleges and universities require a minimum score of 80 to qualify to apply and some requiring a score of at least 100, those students who have not achieved at least the minimum score must continue to study and retake the test again and again until they achieve a high enough score to be accepted by the college or university of their choice.

However, that doesn't necessarily mean that the TOEFL iBT is a difficult test. The truth is that the TOEFL iBT is a very simple basic skills test. In fact, the more you simplify the test, the easier it is to earn a high score. How can I say that with such confidence when so many students get low scores? It's easy. With over 12,000 hours of classroom teaching and all of my students now attending or graduating from major US universities, the TOEFL Master methods are proven to work. Through this book you will learn that the TOEFL iBT is simply a test of structure, procedures and rules. It tests your ability to understand common academic passage structures and sentences as well as certain study skills like finding the main idea, listening and note taking. It also requires students to respond to questions using those structures and certain procedures. Once you've mastered those skills, taking the TOEFL iBT is easy!

Another problem most students face is that they believe the TOEFL iBT is testing their English grammar abilities when actually the test is simply measuring how well a student knows how to take the test. What do I mean by that? The TOEFL iBT is based on rules, structures, and procedures. So, knowing HOW to take the test will raise your score even more than how well you know English grammar.

In this book, you will find that everything had been simplified as much as possible. This book makes **very** complicated things seem easy. Simplifying things not only makes students look smarter, but feel smarter too. By using the techniques taught in this book, not only will you feel smarter and look smarter, pretty soon you will become smarter. Once you learn the structures, processes, and procedures for answering the questions in each section, you will find that the TOEFL iBT is actually not so difficult at all.

The goal of this book is to simplify a very difficult test. You may sometimes find the instructions strange and quite different from the ways you have been learning in the past. Keep in mind that this is NOT regular school and the TOEFL iBT is NOT like tests you have taken in regular school. To pass this test, and the others like it given in colleges and universities, you must learn new ways of test taking.

In the first lesson, you will learn how to understand passage structures, sentence structures, basic techniques for simplifying sentences, how to deal with difficult vocabulary and to follow the logical flow of ideas. Understanding these five things will enable you to quickly find and understand the information you need to answer the questions quickly and accurately.

Moreover, you will learn how to identify question types, quickly find the one sentence in the passage at answers the question and how to eliminate wrong choices according to the rules of the test (POE). Mastering these skills will enable toy to earn a high score with no stress.

**NOTE:** In my attempt to simplify these lessons, I sometimes may not explain things fully enough for some students to understand. However, before you give up, follow the instructions and apply them to the assignments in the ways they are explained. Remember, this is not a regular test and the instructions may seem strange until you learn how to use them. After working out the exercises, if you still feel that you need more explanation, please e-mail me at william.pgila.com for more information.

## WHY TAKE THE TOEFL iBT?

Taking the TOEFL iBT is the first major step in qualifying to apply for entrance into a major college or university. This is an important decision in your life and should be done with serious thought and consideration. Up until this point in your life you have likely lived in a home with family to provide for your food, clothing, and shelter needs. It is easy to take such things for granted when you are born with them and have never known life without them. However, at this point in your life you are now an adult with the responsibilities of caring for yourself. The decisions you make from this day forward will determine the course and the quality of your life. Making such decisions is difficult if not impossible when you have no idea of what successful path to take. Do not worry, I have good news. Although you are growing up and moving out on your own, you are not alone. Many people will be there to help you along the way. Listen to your counselors and advisors at the university or college that you attend. They will give you good advice. One more source that will help you determine your path to success is the biographies of those successful people who are doing the thing that you want to do. There is a saying among successful people, "If you want to be successful, look around you to those who are already successful and emulate them." Another saying states, "If you do what other people do, you will have what other people have." Just remember, no matter what career you choose, becoming successful takes work.

See Chapter 5 for more information on becoming successful.

# Chapter 3 – Speaking Section Overview

Although the Speaking section of the TOEFL iBT is the shortest section of the test with a total testing time of only 20 minutes, it by far causes the most anxiety. In all the years of teaching students how to earn a high score on this section, I've learned that there a few common problems that can be easily overcome with some understanding of what is expected as a response and a little practice.

This book not only gives specific descriptions to the question types and the rules that graders will use to score your responses, it gives you some very good tips in how to control your nerves, organize your speech, minimize common speech mistakes and even how to overcome a strong accent.

You may have noticed that this book is very direct and straight to the point. I have taught students from Chile, Peru, Argentina, Ecuador, Venezuela, Uruguay, Brazil, Bolivia, China, Korea, Vietnam, Japan, Mexico, Panama, Iran, and Saudi Arabia. With over 12,000 hours of teaching, I still find it funny that everyone thinks their problem is unique or different. Although my students may speak different languages, I have found that they all have a few things in common.

1. Nervousness - No one wants to sound stupid.
2. Fear - No one wants to make any mistakes and receive a low score.
3. Confusion - It is difficult to speak when you don't understand the passages or know what graders want to hear.
4. Overcoming an Accent - Some languages make pronouncing words in English difficult, but there are ways to overcome any challenges.

The TOEFL Master's Guide directly addresses each of these issues and offers proven methods to overcome them. Please take the time to read about and practice the methods taught in this book. These methods have worked for all of my students and are sure to work for you as well.

# Chapter 4 – Bridging the Gap

Everyone has a dream of what they want in life, but few people achieve their dreams. The fact is that more people in life fail through lack of desire and poor planning than lack of ability.

I call this chapter "Bridging the Gap" because there is a gap between our dreams and reality, and bridging that gap takes work. By work I mean study and practice. In my experience, too many students want to know but don't want to study, and too many want to be experts but don't want to practice. Ultimately such students live lives of disappointment. However, by studying and practicing the methods in this book you will be acquiring skills needed to be successful at anything you want to do.

DON'T SKIP READING THIS CHAPTER!!

The first things discussed in my classes are the most important things any student needs to know about passing the TOEFL iBT. In general, what most students want to know about is just what it takes to pass the test, but more students fail for reasons other than knowing English well and test taking skills than you might think. Addressing these issues up front has proven to help TOEFL Master students become more serious about practicing and not only earning high scores on their test but becoming more successful in university and life.

Most of us have family asking things like, "What do you want to be when you grow up?" As children we answer with things like, a doctor, lawyer, fireman... or President... the things children dream of being but rarely live up to those dreams. So why ask us? What parents and grandparents, aunts and uncles really want to know is if we have any plans for our lives. However, although asking what we want to be when we grow up is a valid question, it isn't really relevant to our success. What they really should be asking is what kind of lifestyle you want to live when you grow up. For example: if you want to have a family, live in a large house in an upscale neighborhood and drive a BMW, travel and wear expensive clothes you need to have the education and career that will pay for those things. Furthermore, you must be aware what certain careers pay. One of the most common career goals is that of an engineer or architect. Those are very good careers to have and pay well for those who are devoted to the trade and stay with it a long time, but it doesn't start out paying over $100,000 a year with a two year college degree. You must consider that to make a six figure income, your career field will take you at least six years of university education and then another ten years of hard work to get to that level of income. This is the reason the TOEFL Master says, "The money flows to the workers!"

In my experience, knowing **why** you want to go to university is the first thing you need to address. There is a saying, "When the why is big enough, the how doesn't matter." In other words, what is motivating you to put forth so much effort over the next four to six years of your life? Let's face it, what you are doing isn't easy and you had better have a strong motivator to keep you going. Your education may afford you all the things you've ever dreamed of having, but you must define that dream before you get started. All things in this life have a cost and you must take these costs into consideration before you set out to get them. Keep in mind that you can live any kind of lifestyle you want, just please consider carefully what you want in life and make a proper plan to get it.

So, before you move on, seriously consider the answers to these questions and write your answers on paper so that they become real to you:

1. What kind of lifestyle do you want to live?
2. Do you want to get married or stay single? If married, at what age will you get married?
3. Do you want to have a children? If so, how many children would you like to have? How old will you be when you have children?
4. What style of house do you want to live in? Be specific. Write about what the house will be like including the size, number of bedrooms, bathrooms and size of kitchen. What will the property be like your house sits on? Is it in the country, city or the suburbs?
5. What kind of vehicle will you drive? Will you have more than one vehicle?
6. What style of clothing will you wear? Will you have a large or small wardrobe? Will you buy new clothing often?
7. Will you eat at home or at restaurants more?
8. Will you travel or go on vacation each year?
9. What type of entertainment do you like?
10. What is the cost of your education?

All of these things have a cost that must be considered before deciding on a career and the direction of your education. The TOEFL Master strongly advises you to do a search regarding the cost of the lifestyle you want to live and then search for the average income level of those in your chosen career field. For example, many of my students want to be industrial engineers thinking that it is a very important job and must make a lot of money. The truth is that the job of an industrial engineer is important and may pay well in ten years for those who continue to master themselves in it. However, an engineer starting out makes around $48,000 a year. So, as an industrial engineer just starting out of university, after taxes you would take home around $34,500. On that salary you will likely not be living in a mansion, driving a new Mercedes and vacationing in Rio. What's my point? Follow your dream. If it is an engineer you want to be I encourage you to be the best at it. Just consider the reality first so that you are prepared rather than disappointed. By the way, a senior industrial engineer makes around $80,000 annually or more. With that kind of money you could live very well. Be what you want to be and remember, "The money flows to the workers!"

# Chapter 5 – Path to Success

*"Every path leads somewhere. Choose the path that leads to where you want to go and stay on it. Along the way you will find your success."* - William E. Hearn

For example, my path in life led me to write this book in the hope that the instruction of certain techniques will enable you to pass the TOEFL iBT, so that you may move on with your life. The path to success must begin with a purpose in mind. Passing the TOEFL iBT is all for nothing if you do not have a purpose for your life.

The TOEFL Master is no stranger to success, and I have made it my purpose to help you to reach a greater level of achievement in your own life. And so, I offer you this path to success.

## LIFE LESSON #1

*"Look at a homeless person living on the street and consider that it is the choices they make every day that keep them there. Regardless of your family, or of how much money your family may have, if you make the same decisions every day that a homeless person makes, you too will live the life of a homeless person. Conversely, if that same homeless person made the same decisions that you are making every day, they would be where you are now: doing what you are doing right now. The decisions you make matter. You are the master of your own life"*
- William E. Hearn

## DEFINITION OF SUCCESS

First of all, to reach any destination, you must know where you are going. Otherwise you may end up in a place you had not intended to go. Therefore, in order to become successful, you must know what success is. Most people think that success is reaching some kind of goal. They think that means owning a large, fancy house, an expensive car, fine jewelry, and having lots of money. Although it may be true that many successful people have those things . . . those things are not what constitute success. They are merely by-products of a successful life. What then is success? The best definition I've heard of success is this; "Success is the progressive realization of a worthy ideal." Think about that statement for a moment. What does it mean? What does "the progressive realization" mean? Quite simply, "progressive" means "ongoing continuous improvement," and the word "realization" means "to bring forth from a concept of the mind into reality." The words "worthy ideal" simplified mean choose a career that you will enjoy for your life as well as something that benefits many others. In other words, the best idea you can think of that will benefit the most people. Keep in mind that the income you receive for your efforts comes from other people. The more people you can help, the more income you will receive. Consider who the wealthiest man in the world is at the moment: Carlos Slim Helu from Mexico. What makes he and his family so wealthy? They own Telecom and thus provide worldwide cellular communication. Is that what really makes this family so rich? That they sell cell phones? No. They help people stay connected to the ones they love. That is their "worthy ideal." What's yours?

## PERCEPTION
*"Perceived reality is often more believable than actual reality."* - William E. Hearn

What does this statement mean? It means that our perceptions are often more real to us than the true reality that is occurring around us. Some people believe that reality is different for different people, and that it is all a matter of perspective. But, the truth is that our perception does not make reality. For example: A person may try to start a car, but the car won't start. That person may believe the car is possessed by a spirit, or that the car doesn't like them when the true reality is that the battery cables are corroded and not allowing electricity to get to the starter. One could argue that it was an evil spirit that corroded the cables, but in true reality it was oxidation at work.

But, I am not here to argue religion or any belief system. I am giving you sound advice on keeping your feet on the path to success by pointing out that what you believe and the actions that you make matter. Therefore you must be especially aware of how you perceive reality.

What does perception have to do with taking the TOEFL iBT and success? To explain that to you I must explain how the mind works.

## HOW THE MIND WORKS—TWO MINDS
*"Whatever we plant in our subconscious mind and nourish with repetition and emotion will one day become a reality."* - Earl Nightingale

You will discover that the information in each lesson is repeated often in this book. The same thing will be repeated again and again and again. There is a very good reason for this. This course was designed to work with the way the human mind works.

To explain: Humans basically have "two minds." We have a "conscious mind" and a "sub-conscious mind."

First, we have the conscious mind. The conscious mind is a kind of filter. It determines what is true and what is not true. It also decides what is useful to us personally and what isn't. The sub-conscious mind believes that "everything is true." Once the information gets past the conscious mind it goes into the sub-conscious where the learning happens. Learning, by the way, is the process of storing information for future recall.

Therefore, the first time the conscious mind hears something new, the information is "alien" and the conscious mind rejects it; the information just kind of bounces off of our head. The second time the conscious mind hears the same information, it recognizes and categorizes the information as familiar in the subconscious. If someone were to ask you at that time if you know what the information is about, you might say, "Yes." However, when asked to explain the information you would probably say, "I know it. I just can't explain it." This is because the information is only familiar to your sub-conscious mind. Your sub-conscious mind has not yet actually received and learned enough information to be serviceable to you. The third time your mind hears the same information, your mind says to itself, "This might be important" and begins listening to hear if the information is repeated again. The fourth time your mind hears the same information it begins to decide how the information can be used and creates categories in your sub-conscious for information retrieval. The information is then categorized and stored to be used when the information is needed for a useful purpose. The fifth time the mind hears the same information it determines how the information can be used.

At this time the mind is ready to begin learning. From now on, all similar or related information goes directly into the sub-conscious to be used for associated tasks.

Between the sixth and tenth times the sub-conscious mind hears the same information, it figures out the different ways the information can be applied to different circumstances. After processing the information ten times, the mind can now use the information with some regularity of accuracy.

After practicing with the same (or similar) type of information ten times, the mind really begins to make excellent use of the information. From the eleventh to the fiftieth time the mind uses the information, it learns how to use and manipulate the information towards a practical use in many similar but different circumstances. By the time you have seriously practiced something fifty times, the mind will be capable of answering questions using the information with about 80 percent consistent accuracy. By the time the subconscious mind has worked with the information one hundred times it is likely to be an expert in all the different ways the information can be applied and can work with nearly 100 percent consistent accuracy. (This is assuming that the person learning paid attention in the beginning and was careful in learning all the information accurately.) How again, is this relevant to you?

Well, many lessons in this book are very different from what you have learned in the past and so will be alien to you when you first read them. The second time you read them, they will seem familiar to you and you may think that you know and understand them. Don't stop there thinking that you know what to do! In order to score well on the TOEFL iBT, you must read and follow the instructions and learn the rules over and over again at least five times so that you may apply them the right way consistently. From there, you would do well to practice applying the lessons to doing your work one hundred times. The more you practice, the higher your score. With the knowledge of how to take the test and sufficient practice, you may achieve a score high on the TOEFL iBT.

## SELF TALK

A very famous, and perhaps wildly successful man said, *"Whether you think you can or can't—you're right."* — Henry Ford

Be careful when talking to yourself. Now that you have read about how the mind works, understand that our personal thoughts go straight to our subconscious mind, and that whatever we tell ourselves we believe to be true.

Some people will tell you that only crazy people talk to themselves. However, that's not true. Crazy people talk to other people in their minds. Successful people know the secret that you must constantly talk to yourself and evaluate your position in life as well as your state of mind. Napoleon Hill, perhaps one of the most renowned authors of personal success literature said, "What the mind of man can conceive and believe, it can achieve.".

In other words, you must take care as to what you believe, and talking to yourself is a way of programming your beliefs in such a way as to achieve success.

Also, be careful not to accept others' comments that you are not good enough or smart enough to succeed. There will be plenty of them. Sometimes, even members of your own family or your closest friends, well meaning as they might be, will plant negative thoughts in your mind that may prevent you from achieving a high level of success if you listen to them and believe what they tell you. So, cast out any thoughts that you might have that will cause you to sabotage your own life, and talk to yourself in order to continuously evaluate what your beliefs are. Believe that you will succeed. Do the necessary practice to succeed, and you will!

## STAY FOCUSED

*"To conquer frustration, one must remain intensely focused on the outcome, not the obstacles."* — T.F. Hodge

One of the most difficult things to do in life today is to stay focused. With so many distractions and duties pulling us in different directions, it is no wonder that we have a difficult time learning. However, in order to become successful you must learn and practice focusing on what is in front of us at the moment. We must see the problem but focus on the solution.

When learning, our brains work much like a computer. If the information coming in is corrupted it won't be any good. Think about downloading a program. If the download is corrupted, what can you do with it? It probably won't even open, and you must delete it because it isn't usable. It's the same thing with putting information into your brain. If the information coming is fragmented or mixed up with other information, you likely won't be able to remember it well. In time your brain will delete the corrupted information and you won't remember it at all.

In order to learn something well so that it is serviceable when you need it, you must focus on what you are learning at the moment. Also, trying to recall information takes time, and the faster you have recall, the more efficient you will be.

You will face many challenges on your path to success. By focusing on the solutions you can solve these challenges quickly and more effectively. This applies to the TOEFL iBT because you will be dealing with answering questions on a timed test. Each question type requires a special procedure or structure to be answered. You will not have time to second guess yourself, and therefore must remain focused on each question to answer it quickly and correctly.

## DISCIPLINE

*"We must all suffer one of two things: the pain of discipline or the pain of regret or disappointment."* - Jim Rohn

Every successful person has discipline in their lives. There are two types of discipline you must master to be successful. One type of discipline is defined as an activity, exercise, or a regimen that improves a skill. The other is defined as a behavior in accordance with rules of conduct. To maintain these types of discipline, successful people develop "successful habits."

To achieve a state of success in life, you must develop certain "successful habits." It is said that "consistency is the key to longevity." Thus, the secret key to a successful life is consistency. Great success in life is merely the consistent application of successful habits. To be successful you must create certain habits in your life that will carry you through each day, even at times when you do not feel that you are capable of going on.

Building successful habits takes the first type of discipline. You must be consistent at doing a certain thing for twenty–one days straight. If at any time you do not perform the activity during those twenty–one days, you must begin again. And so you must maintain the first type of discipline in order to build successful habits. Once you have developed a habit you must maintain it through the second type of discipline. You must have a set of rules that you follow consistently.

Let's face it. Life is hard sometimes and we don't always like getting up and going to work. We don't really enjoy practicing something for hours on end, and we aren't always in a good mood. It is in these times of our lives that successful habits will carry us through. On those days when, no matter how much you are being paid, you just don't feel like going to work, successful habits will get you out of bed, showered, dressed, and onward to a successful day.

How will this help you to achieve a high score on the TOEFL iBT?

The TOEFL iBT is not like regular tests that you are used to taking in school. The questions each have a very specific structure and procedure for answering them. Once you have disciplined yourself to following those structures and procedures consistently, you will habitually achieve a high score.

# STAYING PREPARED

*"**Fortune favors the prepared mind.**"* - Louis Pasteur

If you want to be successful in life you must prepare for success and stay prepared. Here is a little story to illustrate my point.

Many years ago when trees were cut down by lumber-jacks, men who cut down trees with a hand held axe, there was one lumber-jack who was famous for his ability to cut more trees than anyone in all the land. For over twenty years he held this honor, but as with anyone with such a reputation, eventually a challenger would come to take his title.

One year a very tall, large and muscular young man came looking to make a name for himself and sought out this legendary lumber-jack to challenge him to just such a contest. He searched for a great giant of a man in a forest where he had heard the legend was working. Finally he came upon an unimpressive looking man who was resting under the shade of a massive oak with his axe laying across his lap. This man was exceptionally ordinary looking. He was only five feet eight inches tall and seemed to blend into the scenery. The young challenger asked the man if he knew where to find the legendary lumber-jack, and the older man replied, "You're looking at him." The young man was obviously surprised as he stood staring, speechless and with his mouth open. "I get that a lot.", said the older man.

Once the mountain of a young man recovered his wits, he challenged the legend to the contest, and so they began. The young man began chopping furiously and soon wood chips were flying in all directions. He worked feverishly striking with mighty blows that echoed throughout the forest. One tree after another fell to his might and axe, and he was sure that the contest was his.

Toward mid-day, the young man looked up to see what progress the old man was making and saw him chopping steadily at a tree. However, a little while later the old man was resting under a tree just as he was at their first meeting. The young man thought to himself, "Legend, huh? He looks like a tired old man. I'll cut down twice as many trees today as him." Throughout the rest of the day the young man kept looking up only to see the old man resting by a different tree.

Finally, the end of the day came and it was time to determine the winner of the contest. The smug young man was about worn out from the work but sure of his victory as he counted off loudly the number of trees he fell, "One! - Two! - Three! - Four! - Five! - Six! - Seven! - Eight! Beat that old man!" Surely that was an amazing number as the average that any man could do was three. Silently, the old legend took inventory of the trees that went down under his axe that day. Ten . . . ten trees lay on the ground just as sure as the sun rises in the morning.

"Impossible! That can't be!", bellowed the young man barely regaining his breath from the exertion of the day. The old legend smiled and quietly asked, "Why do you say that?" The young man blinked. The old man wasn't even winded. In fact he looked as if he could chop down another ten trees before retiring for the night. The young man was daunted and, after calming a little, said, "Each time I looked over you were resting under a tree while I never stopped once.

How did you do it? How did you beat me?" A knowing smile crept up into the old legends face and se simply said, "What you didn't see was that, as I sat resting, I was sharpening my axe, and with each stroke I hit the soft spot of the tree." - End.

Do you see? Although the young man worked very hard without stopping, the old man was prepared by understanding how to cut the trees with the least effort, and he stayed prepared by resting between work yet always preparing for the next time his skills were needed.

The moral of this story? Be sure to educate yourself well in the field you intend to work, and always continue to practice improving your abilities. Work smart - not hard.

## RESPONSIBILITY

Responsibility is just what the word implies—your ability to respond. It means more than simply making the right decision at the right time and taking appropriate action. It is about accepting accountability and being able to handle situations in a mature and effective way.

We are not naturally born with the ability to respond effectively to every situation. We must become educated in many things and have experience in those things before being responsible. One thing that successful people know is that they don't always make the right decisions, but when mistakes are made, the responsibility for correcting the situation is theirs.

To be successful, you must develop the ability to respond effectively to different situations. To do this, you must have an ongoing education and a life of experience.

## RELATIONSHIPS

*"No Man Is An Island"* - John Donne

No person can nor has ever become successful alone. To become successful, we must build relationships with those people who share a common vision with us and we must also have the sense to maintain the relationships of integrity.

To build successful relationships, a person needs three things: Trust, Trust, and Trust. First, you must gain and hold the trust of people. If people don't trust you personally, they will have nothing to do with you. Second, people must trust that the product or service you are providing is as advertised and is a good value for their money. If your product or service proves otherwise, you will eventually lose your business. Finally, people must be able to trust themselves. When a person loses confidence in their own ability to trust themselves, they lose the ability to say "yes" or "no" with confidence. If a person can't say, "yes" with certainty, they are most certainly saying, "no."

To have and maintain successful relationships, you must be honest with people as well as yourself. With such honesty, people will continue to trust you and you will continue to be successful.

## LIFE LESSON #2

*"Little things become big things. A drop of water alone is barely noticed but becomes a summer rain when joined with other drops. A speck of soil alone serves no one but in abundance becomes a fertile field. A grain of corn alone feeds no one but join these three together and in time you will have an abundant land growing food enough to feed everyone."* - William E. Hearn

## DEVOTION

*"Make small promises . . . and keep them."* —William E. Hearn

What is devotion? Devotion is your ability to fulfill a promise to do something: to dedicate yourself to a certain cause or purpose. Successful people have chosen for themselves a purpose that they feel is worthy of their very lives. They dedicate all they are and have to their purpose through devotion. The most common form of devotion is that of a married couple and as parents.

Most people live their lives going to their jobs day after day without truly being devoted to their work. They go simply because they need the money for the food they eat, clothes they wear, and a place to sleep while they wait to get up and go back to work again. No matter how much they are paid, they live a life of poverty. This is not devotion.

Devotion is the commitment to a greater purpose that will carry you to success. To be successful you must make promises and keep them, and that is not easy to do. Many people in this world make great promises and never follow through, as it is extremely difficult to keep great promises. There are simply too many unforeseen variables. Many more people make even the smallest of promises, and still they do not keep their words. Have you ever had someone tell you that they will call you, and they don't? Or, have you ever had someone ask you to a movie, or to go out to eat at a certain time, and you were really looking forward to going? However, when that time came, they didn't show up or even call? Then, you finally get up the courage to call them only to discover that they had forgotten all about you! How does that make you feel? Maybe you shrug it off and say, "That's okay," but inside you are hurting. You might think that person is a jerk, or worse, you might wonder what is wrong with you that they forgot about you. Either way, you have lost a bit of your ability to trust. Now, you don't really trust that person, and worse, you don't trust yourself for having been made a fool of.

If you want to be successful in life today, "Make small promises . . . and keep them." The people who cannot be trusted in small things will not be trusted in greater things. So, make small promises and keep them! In this people will learn that they can trust you.

Trust is a secret key to achieving great success.

## LIFE LESSON #3

*"Never compare yourself to someone else. There will always be someone smarter or dumber, richer or poorer, faster or slower, taller or shorter, prettier or uglier . . . comparing yourself to others will only give you a false sense of either superiority or inferiority. The only person you can honestly compare yourself to is the person you used to be."* - William E. Hearn

## RESPECT

*"This **above all**: to thine ownself be true,"* - William Shakespeare

What is respect? We know that we should respect our parents and elders. We should respect the law. We know that we exhibit different behaviors when around those people that we respect. We act accordingly to what people expect of us in certain situations. But, is that respect? Everyone wants respect, but few know how to give it. Perhaps that is because few even know what respect is. **Respect is a reflection**. Literally, respect means, "looking back." Therefore the best way to learn about respect is to begin by respecting yourself (self-respect). Take the time now to take a good look at yourself and to discover just who you are what you truly believe. Write down on paper a constitution for yourself. List what your strong beliefs are: The things that you will do no matter what, and the things that you would never do no matter what. Also, make a list of the things that you might do but are conditional. Once you have a good understanding of yourself, you will begin to see others more clearly. Therefore, instead of demanding respect from others, maybe what we should be striving for is "consideration for one another." With such consideration, respect is a naturally occurring thing.

## OVERCOMING FEAR

Everyone feels fear. Those who refuse to admit that they have fears have in fact the fear of appearing weak. Every brave person who ever lived has been brave only because they felt fear and acted responsibly in the face of it. Do not be ashamed to feel fears, as it is a natural part of life. Only recognize the fear you have, and act responsibly when you feel it.

The six major fears are: The fear of poverty, the fear of criticism, the fear of illness, the fear of loneliness, the fear of old age, and the fear of death. In our youth we feel the first two listed fears more than the others. Moreover, many feel the fear of criticism the most. The fear of criticism is a major cause of most failures in the lives of young people. This fear often manifests itself in the form of procrastination and/or low test scores caused by what we call test anxiety.

## OVERCOMING TEST ANXIETY

Test anxiety is a common problem for many students who take the TOEFL iBT. There are four main fears that students experience that primarily cause test anxiety. They include: the fear of the unknown, the fear of failure, the fear of criticism, and the fear of loss.

First, the fear of the unknown comes from simply not knowing what to do in a general sense, not knowing what to expect on the test, or that we don't know what is expected from us to pass the test.

With the fear of the unknown, we ask ourselves questions such as, "What if I don't know enough about the subjects to answer the questions right?" or, "What if I can't answer the questions in the time given?" or, "What if I don't know what some of the words mean?" or, "What kind of test is it?", "Do I have to write the answers out, or is it a multiple choice test?", "Will I have to talk during the test?", and so on. . . .

Fear of the unknown causes many students to experience anxiety and may cause some students to procrastinate in taking the TOEFL iBT, meaning that they will continuously "wait and take it later," or it could even cause some students to never take the test at all.

The TOEFL Master Book helps students to overcome the fear of the unknown easily by giving simple instructions and familiarizing them with every aspect of the test. Reading the tutorials and taking the practice tests in this course will thoroughly prepare you for taking and passing the TOEFL iBT with a high score.

Another aspect of the fear of the unknown comes from the fear of relocating to a strange new place. Many students worry about what the new school will be like. They worry about whether or not will they fit in, or if the other students will like them. Worries persist about whether or not they speak English well enough to get good grades in their classes or if they will be able to communicate with other students to make friends. There are so many unknown things about moving to a different country, how can a student possibly overcome those fears?

It is necessary to address them and dismiss them one at a time.

Fears are cowards, and when we face them they run away.

Take for example the fear that we will not fit in—that we may not be accepted by others. This is the same fear every new student feels before their first day of school anywhere. Whether it was you're beginning of Kindergarten, or your initial day of high school, you have already faced and overcome the same old fear again and again. Yet, here we are preparing for university life with all those old fears behind us and you are still afraid. Why? What was true of the past is the same for the future. Don't worry about fitting in. There is a place for everyone and you will find yours. People all over the world have the same fears. Maybe someone you are about to meet is afraid and wondering if you will like them? As far as speaking English well enough goes, maybe you might have some problems at first, but you will get better every day as you are surrounded by English-speaking people and things to read. Most people don't learn English very well or quickly because they only hear or read English for the short time they are in their English classes—usually two or three hours a week. However, being constantly surrounded by English speakers will help you learn and use your English faster than you ever could anywhere else. In other words, don't worry. Just go and have fun. The rest will come naturally.

The other fears are a bit more complex and are somewhat difficult (but not impossible) to overcome. Let's address them one at a time so that you can understand better how they affect your abilities and therefore know how to overcome them.

The so-called fear of failure has been a debilitating fear for many test takers. Not just for the TOEFL iBT, but for all important tests students must take. There is even a clinical disability consideration for students who genuinely face this fear and simply cannot take a test because of it. However, although the fear of failure is common, and sometimes prevents students from taking or doing well on a test, it is really quite easy to overcome.

There are several aspects of the fear of failure. The most common aspect often comes from not knowing what will be on the test (fear of the unknown). Yet, this aspect, of course, is easily overcome by learning about the test and practicing until you get good at taking it. Another aspect of this type of fear comes from being worried about what people will say to us, or say to others about us, if we do not get a high enough score on the test. This is known as the "fear of criticism."

The fear of criticism is the fear that certain people will ridicule us or unjustly criticize us for not meeting their standards. Often, students believe that, if they do not perform as well as they want to, or as well as others (such as family and friends) think they should, they will be criticized for their failure. We also sometimes place this fear upon ourselves when we don't live up to our own expectations. Regardless, the fear of criticism may cause a person to shut out anyone or anything that will cause them to feel bad about themselves. This fear has even been known to cause people to sabotage their own test (answer questions with the wrong choices even though they know the right one) just to escape the anxiety they feel. They will say, "It doesn't matter. I answered wrongly on purpose" to justify their failure. This type of anxiety can sometimes even prevent students from taking the test at all. The best way to overcome this fear is to learn the structure and rules for getting a high score on the test and then practicing until you are confident that you can get the score you need on the actual test. Working to do well and building confidence in your abilities is the key to overcoming many fears, including the fear of failure and the fear of criticism.

Finally, the fear of loss (sometimes known as the fear of success) can be equally devastating. The fear of loss comes to us when we are afraid of losing our familiar, comfortable surroundings. Admit it; moving to a strange country can be quite intimidating. Just thinking of the many things we'll have to face alone can make us want to crawl back into bed and stay there. Speaking of crawling back into bed, your bed is something that you will miss. Your room, with all of your personal possessions, is really a comfort zone to you. This is the place you go for relief from the outside world. It's your "safe" place. You will miss your room and all of the things in it. Your parents, family, and friends will all be absent from your life for perhaps the first time. You might not think about it now, but deep inside a fear of losing these familiar things could be causing you great anxiety. This kind of anxiety can cause a person to do crazy things such as failing the TOEFL iBT on purpose, or putting it off to practice enough to attain a "perfect" score. The fear of losing your "comfort zone" is a powerful one. The fear of loss has been known to prevent more people from becoming successful or limiting their ability to become more successful than any other fear.

So, how do you overcome this fear? Well it is overcome in stages. First, you must realize that you have the fear and acknowledge it for what it is: that is, an irrational emotion. Next, you must face this fear in a logical way. One thing you can do is to remind yourself that going to university is only a temporary thing and that you will be coming back home after graduating. (If that is your plan. Not everyone wants to go back home.) You can also take something small from home with you to university that gives you comfort. It could be something special like a gift given to you by a favorite relative or friend. We call this taking a piece of home and doing this will help you feel more at home in your new life at an American university. Finally, stay in touch with family as much as you can. With the Internet so readily available to most people now it is easier to stay in touch over long distances. If your family does not have a computer, write a letter. In fact, even if your family does have a computer and Internet connection, write a letter anyway. A hand written letter is special. It has far more value than a phone call or an e-mail. Hand-written letters are cherished and read over and over again. If you really love someone . . . write them a letter in your own hand. All of these things will help you to overcome the fear of loss because they help you to stay connected to those you love.

In conclusion, this course can help alleviate test anxiety caused by the fear of the unknown by teaching you how the test is designed, the rules for what is right and wrong on it and exactly how to answer the questions quickly and correctly. This book can also help you overcome the fear of failure and the fear of criticism by helping you to build confidence in your test taking abilities. To overcome these fears, you must simply learn the structure of the test and the procedures for answering the questions, practice them until they become automatic and you will do well on the TOEFL iBT. Finally, the fear of loss is something that you will get over simply by going to the university and getting settled into your room, with your classes, friends, and surroundings. In a short time, your new school will eventually become your new temporary home, and your new friends will be your new family.

Passing the TOEFL iBT is one step to becoming an adult and moving on into your bright future.

NOTE: The **KEY** to confidence and a high score on the TOEFL iBT is PRACTICE, PRACTICE, PRACTICE!!!

# THE VALUE OF WORK
### *"The Money flows to the workers."* - William E. Hearn

You may think that you want to receive a good education in order to get a well-paying job: a job where you will be paid a lot of money. You probably think of printed "money" as the basis of wealth. However, the term "money" likely means something different to those who do not understand how "money" works or even what "money" is.

Allow me to explain what the truly wealthy people around the world know about "money" that the average person does not.

Most people think of money as the currency used to purchase goods and/or services, often in the form of paper bills and metal coins. It is something they can count and put in their pocket or a bank. When their hands are full, they think that they have a lot of it—money. This type of "money" is actually a bartering tool. In the past, people bartered, or traded things they had for the goods or services they wanted or needed. It was easy to exchange things like corn for tomatoes, or a basket filled with wheat for a day's use of a mule. However, as societies became more complex and goods and services became more diverse, it became difficult to make these easy trades. For example, a farmer may need a new tractor, but all he has to trade is the corn in his field. Thus, he goes to the man who sells tractors to make a trade, but the tractor dealer doesn't like or want that much corn. Another example could be that the man who deals in tractors needs an eye operation, so he goes to the eye doctor for help and offers to trade a tractor for the operation, but the doctor doesn't want or need a tractor. You can see the dilemma here. What is needed is a form of a universal bartering tool. Thus "money" has taken that form. Using this bartering tool known as cash (money), the farmer sells his corn and uses the cash he has received to purchase the tractor. The tractor dealer in turn uses the cash received from the farmer to pay the doctor for an eye operation. Regardless of the form of payment, it is still essentially bartering.

In addition, the definition that wealthy people use for money is altogether different. Money is the process of translating a thought in the mind to a product or service that can then be converted to cash for trade. In other words, "money" is the idea. Think about it.

What is the most valuable thing you can own? Is it a car, or a house? The value of those or any tangible thing, is limited to its perceived value, and once it has been sold is no longer of value to you. But, intellectual property (the idea) of something can bring ongoing wealth until the end of your days. An author can write a book once and print and sell a virtually unlimited number of copies. The value of one good idea is far greater than any material product. Everything you can set your eyes or lay your hands on started out as an idea in someone's head. Every piece of paper, every pencil, every computer, cell phone . . . you name it, started out as an idea, and if you want a piece of that idea you must pay for it. Thus, the value of any idea is directly related to one's ability to translate it into a physical product or service.

Now, what does all of this have to do with the value of work?

Just as the term money has two different meanings, so too does the term work. What is work? To most, work is going to do a job at a place of employment. It is the physical labor one performs to earn a paycheck. This form of work has a very limited ability to provide an ongoing income. In fact, given this definition, as soon as the work stops so stops the income.

In contrast, the real definition of work for the wealthy is this: Work is the translation of an idea into a reality-based product or service. In other words, work is the process of taking an abstract idea from your mind and creating a physical product or service. To be able to take an abstract idea from your mind and create a real product takes education and effort. You must know everything about the product or service that you intend to make real. Then you must master every process that it takes to manifest that product or idea into a reality. Getting an education and developing that knowledge takes time, and utilizing that knowledge takes work. The more education you have, the better able you are to have ideas of value and the ability to translate them into a reality where they can then be converted into cash. To put it another way, "Work is the bridge that spans the gap between your dreams and reality."

## LIFE LESSON #3
*"There is a direct correlation between output and income. If you doubt it, simply sit down for thirty days and do nothing. It won't be long before everything you have, including your health, is taken away."* - William E. Hearn

## HIGHER EDUCATION
*"We cannot make decisions about things we don't know about."* - William E. Hearn

What is an education for? To make more money of course, right? But, how will you make your education earn you a greater income? First, you must understand that it isn't just the degree (the piece of paper) that you hold that earns you more money, it's your ability to use what you've learned to create a valuable product or service that gets the cash. Also, you must understand that intellectual property is the most valuable thing a person can own. In other words, what's in your head is where your money comes from. If your head is empty, your pockets will also be empty.

Getting an education does two things for you. First, it fills your head with ideas, and second, it gives you the ability to manifest those ideas into reality where you can trade them for the things you really want.

To put that into perspective, most careers today require an applicant to have a minimum of a bachelor's degree (4 years) just to apply. Regardless of how smart you are, or how much you know and the amount of experience you have, nothing matters more than the degree you get from an accredited college or university. In most cases, without a degree you won't even get a chance to show someone how good you are at doing the job. Your application simply won't be considered.

Furthermore, there is a direct correlation between the level of education a person has and how much money they earn. For example, high school drop-outs are typically destined to do manual labor jobs that pay only minimum wage, and they will be displaced when there is an applicant who comes along with a high school diploma. Those with less than a high school diploma earn an average income of $22,860 a year. Take out taxes and their annual take home pay is only $18,745. Match that income to the lifestyle you want to have, and you quickly realize that going to university is necessary.

Comparatively, people who have received their Master's degree earn an average of $59,230 a year with a take home pay of $48,569. If you continue to your Doctoral or professional degree the average income is $84,448. That's $71,780 that you take home after taxes. That is nearly four times the earnings of someone who didn't pursue a higher education. But more importantly, the difference is your ability to live your dreams. All people dream of having a successful life filled with the things they want, but those with an education, and the willingness to do what is necessary to have those things, actually get to enjoy them.

Sources: http://nces.ed.gov/fastfacts/display.asp?id=77 and http://www.bls.gov/emp/ep_chart_001.htm

**REMEMBER**: We cannot make decisions regarding things we know nothing about.

## MOTIVATION & INCENTIVE

There is a very true saying among the ultra-successful: "When the 'Why' is big enough, the 'How' will take care of itself." Have you taken the time to seriously ask yourself why you are taking the TOEFL iBT exam? I mean, other than to fulfill a requirement needed to attend an English-speaking university, have you asked yourself, "Why?"

Although you may not think of it now, this questions "why?" is perhaps the most important determiner of your ultimate success in life. This question provides the foundation of your dreams
and is the incentive for your becoming successful. Without the "why?" the cosmos has no motivation to support your dream.

Perhaps you haven't asked yourself this all important question yet while things are going rather well if not at least moving along . . . but I can assure you that this question will become paramount in your mind when things get difficult. The lack of a significant answer to the question "why?" is tantamount to quitting.

Therefore, the TOEFL Master **STRONGLY** urges you to ask yourself "WHY?" Why am I doing this? Why am I going to an English-speaking university in a foreign country? Why am I working so hard?"

Make a list of "why?" questions, and write down your answers. Make certain that they are YOUR answers and not the wishes or expectations of someone else.

**Remember**: When your "why" is big enough, the "how" will take care of itself.

# THE POWER OF WRITING THINGS DOWN
*"If it isn't in writing it doesn't exist."* - Unknown

As a general rule, 90 percent of the people in the world control 10 percent of the wealth, while 10 percent of the people control 90 percent of the wealth. And 1 percent of the people control **ALL** of the world's wealth. If this were true, what percent of the population do you want to be in? A better question would be, "What does this 1 percent have in common that the other 99 percent doesn't?" To answer that question let's take a look at who theses three groups are. The 90 per centers are the common people. They are your workers:

Those who labor for a paycheck and those who strive to live however they may. This group works themselves to death striving to survive on 10 percent of the world's wealth. The 10 per centers are the managers. This group consists mainly of educated people who use what they have read (learned) in order to manage others to get the production work done. They typically have paid for their education and are held accountable for the production work. If they are top level managers, they have a say in writing company policies, and often get an income bonus for keeping costs low and production at a high level. Most of them live comfortably well. And then there is the 1 percent: Those who control all of the world's wealth. This group has one thing in common that the others do not share. They write everything down. They are your corporation owners, politicians, lawyers, judges, and to a lesser extent professors. Corporation owners employ the 90 percent and determine what they will get paid as well as the cost of goods and services. Politicians, lawyers, and judges create all of the laws and regulations that the rest of us live by, while professors write the books that the rest of us are educated by. In other words, this group controls everything.

If you intend to be one of the 1 percent—good for you, I hope you enjoy yourself and remember that I helped in my small way to help get you there.

If, and highly likely, you intend to be in the 10 percent of the population who controls 90 percent of the wealth, welcome to the party. Just remember that the money flows to the workers, so take this course seriously, develop successful habits and practice until you can answer questions automatically using the skills and structures taught in this book.

Regardless which group you find yourself in, get into the habit of writing things down. Keep a journal of your dreams and plans for your future. Make a monthly review of what you have written to determine if you are staying on the track of accomplishing your goals.

One last thing, writing things down is not just for keeping track of your plans and marking your goals. There is a secret power in writing things down. Something happens when we put our dreams on paper. Something magical, mystical, or divine happens when we commit our thoughts to paper. The ultra-wealthy people know this is the ultimate key to success. There is an ancient saying, "If it isn't in writing, it doesn't exist."

Whatever it is you want out of life, write it down. Take a moment now to write down what goals you have for yourself in the next five years. Where do you want to be in your life? All costs aside, what would you like to study? Where would you like to live? What lifestyle would you like to have? What kind of clothes would you like to wear? Would you prefer living in a house or an apartment or condo? What kind of dining do you prefer—to eat at home or a fine restaurant? What kind of car would you like to drive, or will you have someone else drive you? What career would you like to have? Do you want to get married or stay single? Will you get married while you are young, or will you wait until you are older? Will you have a family? Give your life some serious thought and write all your dreams down. Don't worry about how fantastic your thoughts may seem. Remember that every wealthy and successful person in the world began as a newborn baby. Everything they know and have has been added to them since. It is the same for all of us. Write down your dreams and be specific. The more you can define your dream on paper, the more your dreams will become a reality as you envision them. What do you want? Write it down!

# Part II: Speaking Section Made Easy

## Chapter 6 – Speaking Section

## SPEAKING TUTORIAL

The TOEFL iBT Speaking Section tests your ability to understand and respond verbally to common questions and classroom situations as well as conversations encountered on a university campus.

When attending a university in the United States, you will encounter many situations where you must speak to fellow students, professors, administrators and other university personnel. In fact, for some of your classes, class participation may be 30 to 70 percent of your grade. That makes having the ability to speak English very important not just for passing the TOEFL iBT, but for communicating well with classmates and for getting good grades in each course!

Because of this importance, and because it is something few TOEFL students get to practice, the Speaking Section often causes the most anxiety. The TOEFL Master says, "Relax". The Speaking Section is very similar to the other sections in that it is a test of structure and procedures. Once you are familiar with the different passages and the requirements for responding to each one, this section may actually seem easier than the others. Besides, the Speaking Section is only twenty minutes long from start to finish, and you will only speak for a total of 5 ½ minutes of that.

What's more, you only have to speak for either forty-five seconds or one minute for each depending on the question. So, speaking really isn't the biggest part of this section. Other skills you will need are reading comprehension, listening and taking notes. That's right… **the skills you have already mastered** from the Reading and Listening sections are the most important skills needed to score well on the Speaking Section.

NOTE: Anxiety is a coward. Face your anxiety with the knowledge and skills you have mastered and your anxiety will run fast and far away from you.

Below are the tasks that you can expect to master on the TOEFL iBT Speaking Section:

1.  Two Independent Tasks, with one question asking about a personal preference and the other asking you to choose an option or state whether you agree or disagree with a certain statement.

    The time breakdown to complete these two tasks:

    > 15 seconds preparation time
    >
    > 45 second speaking time

2.  Two Integrated Tasks that require you to listen to a conversation or lecture and respond.

    The time breakdown to complete these two tasks:

    > 45 seconds reading time
    > 60 to 90 seconds conversation/lecture
    > 30 seconds preparation time
    > 60 seconds speaking time

3. Two Integrated Tasks that require you to listen to a conversation or lecture and respond.

   The time breakdown to complete these two tasks.
   1 to 2 minute conversation/lecture
   20 seconds preparation time
   60 seconds speaking time

**You will have 20 minutes to complete the entire section.**

## SCORING FOR THE SPEAKING SECTION

The speaking section is graded on a scale of 0 to 4. A score of 0 (zero) is reserved for a response that simply repeats the prompt, does not answer the question, is in a foreign language (any language other than English) or is left blank.

Human beings known as "graders" will be listening to recordings of your speech. The graders for the TOEFL iBT use a grading tool known as a "Rubric". These are simply rules that the graders use to evaluate a test takers response. Because the TOEFL iBT is a standardized test, responses must also be standardized. That means that they must follow certain rules and patterns that can be easily identified and graded.

The grades are given "holistically" based on the rules and then converted to a scaled score. The conversion from holistic to scaled score is listed below.

SPEAKING SECTION SCORING CHART

| Holistic Score | TOEFL Score |
|---|---|
| 4.0 | 30 |
| 3.5 | 27 |
| 3.0 | 23 |
| 2.5 | 19 |
| 2.0 | 15 |
| 1.5 | 11 |
| 1.0 | 8 |
| 0 | 0 |

The Holistic Score is the average of scores from all six speaking tasks. For example, if your first three answers score a "3" and your second three answers score a "4," your holistic score will be 3.5, thus making your *TOEFL* score 27.

ETS has very explicit rules when it comes to speaking responses. You can find them on their web site at: http://www.ets.org/Media/Tests/TOEFL/pdf/Speaking_Rubrics.pdf

## Speaking Section Rubrics (Rules)

### Independent Tasks (Questions 1 and 2)

When graders listen to your responses, and there will actually be human beings listening to and grading your responses, they have the rules of ETS to go by. Nothing is left to interpretation or of how they "feel" about your response. Either you have met a certain criteria or you haven't. It is the only fair and consistent way to grade.

If you took the time to go to the ETS web site, you might have found that the rules are not very easy to interpret?

Don't worry, as with all things, the TOEFL Master likes to simplify things.

Listed below is the simplified version of the Speaking Section Rules for questions 1 & 2.

1.  You must answer all questions in English only.
2.  You must answer the question completely.
3.  Speak (enunciate your words) clearly.
4.  Have no long pauses or extra words interjected such as "uh" or "um".
5.  Give reasons, examples and details that are relative to the topic.
6.  You must use connection words and phrases such as "One reason", "another reason", "for example", and "furthermore".
7.  You must use proper grammar.
8.  You must use the correct vocabulary words.

Sounds like a lot? If so, the TOEFL master has good news! Most students believe that they start out with a score of "0" and must work hard to give a response good enough to receive a score of "4", but the truth is that everyone starts out with a score of "4"! All you have to do is maintain your score. How do you do that? Follow the rules!

In other words, when you have practiced enough to follow the rules and response structures of ETS, and get good at following them, you will score a "4". Points are deducted for not meeting certain criteria. For example, if you give a response that follows all of the rules except that you failed to use connection words and phrases, you will likely score a "3". Furthermore, if you give a response that follows most of the rules but have long pauses, extra words and poor grammar, you will likely score a "2". So, if you want to receive a high score, practice following the rules!

Listed below is the simplified version of the Speaking Section Rules for Questions 3, 4, 5 and 6.

1. You must answer all questions in English only.
2. You must answer the question completely.
3. Speak (enunciate your words) clearly.
4. Have no long pauses or extra words interjected such as "uh" or "um".
5. You must state accurate reasons, examples and details as stated and in the order they appear in the passages.*
6. You must use connection words and phrases such as "One reason", "another reason", "for example", and "furthermore".
7. You must use proper grammar.
8. You must use the correct vocabulary words.

*Notice that the rules are almost the same except for rule number 5 that states you must state *accurate* reasons, examples and details as stated and ***in the order they appear in the passages***. This means that you should take notes while reading and listening to these sections in order to restate the information accurately in the order it appeared in the passages.

# NOTHING TO FEAR

**DON'T TRY TO GIVE A PERFECT RESPONSE!!!** Any time we try to give a "perfect" response, we ultimately screw it up. There is no way you can speak at a level above the one you speak at now without knowing how and practicing it a lot. You are better speaking well at the level you are at now, or learn the grammar and structures needed to give a higher response and practice them until your responses become natural. Even then, speak to your level.

The graders consider three major areas when judging the quality of your response.

1. **Delivery:** On the TOEFL, delivery refers to both the flow and clarity of your speech. A higher-scoring response will be well paced and free of long pauses and unnecessary interjections. Although the speech may contain minor pronunciation errors or problems with intonation, these errors must not detract from the understanding of your speech.

2. **Language Use:** The graders are looking for effective use of grammar and vocabulary. Complexity of sentence structure will also be considered. A higher-scoring response will contain compound sentences: those sentences that join two ideas with a conjunction, and a range of vocabulary. Your response may have a few grammatical errors. Again, the speech does not have to be perfect, but the errors must not affect the listener's ability to understand the speech.

3. **Topic Development:** This includes how well your response addresses the tasks as well as the development of your ideas. The graders are judging you not only on how you speak, but also on what you say. The speaker must make effective use of connection words and phrases. This is an important point because test takers who are comfortable speaking in English may not achieve a top score if they do not structure their responses correctly (the ETS way).

Again, these standards conform to the three basic Core Concept Skills: purpose, main idea and structure.

By now you have noticed a common pattern in each section. Everything written and spoken has the same basic structure – topic, purpose, reasons, examples, details, and conclusion. This is a working formula that remains consistent in every section for a reason. This is how we understand things and how information is presented academically in text books and class lectures.

If you are still having difficulty with your responses, an excellent practice exercise is to write a short speech and then practice speaking it. Use a recorder and play back your speech to hear how you sound. Professional speakers use this exercise regularly.

The best way to score well on this section of the TOEFL iBT is to PRACTICE SPEAKING.

## DEALING WITH AN ACCENT

The good news about the TOEFL iBT is that you can have an accent and still earn a high score! Keep in mind that the Speaking section is **not** testing how well you sound like an American but rather how well your words are understood so that you may communicate effectively. In any language, speaking is about *communication*. In other words, speaking is about how well others understand what you are saying.

The problem with having an accent comes when we have difficulty pronouncing certain words in a way that they are commonly spoken in English. Believe it or not, this isn't a problem for just non-US English speakers. In fact, all throughout the US people speak with different accents. In some area of the Unites States the accent of people is so strong that they being interviewed on national TV need subtitles so that others can understand what is being said. So, having an accent can be a problem with communication.

To earn a high score on the TOEFL iBT the graders must understand what you are saying. So, rather than trying to suppress your accent, let's enhance your ability to enunciate clearly and pronounce words in a way that makes it easy for graders to hear them. Usually this involves simply slowing our speech a little and holding our mouths in a way to make the sounds common to certain words. With a little practice using a recorder you will be speaking clearly enough to earn a high score.

So, how do we overcome a strong accent?

One challenge in speaking well is that we don't hear the sounds or the "emphasis" on certain parts of words. The first thing to do is to break words down into their parts called syllables. In English, words are broken up into syllables, and each syllable has its own sound, and one syllable will have an emphasis. For example: **sophisticated** is pronounced **"su - fis' - ti - kate - ed"** with the emphasis (stress) on the second syllable. This emphasis is part of the English language and must be used in order to be understood well. Therefore, the most important thing is to *hear* the words spoken in English first and then practice repeating them. The TOEFL Master suggests you use an online dictionary that includes recorded pronunciations of words. Look up the words you will use and practice saying them into a recorder and play them back.

Another challenge many people have is pronouncing certain sounds made when speaking words in English. This involves holding your mouth and tongue to make certain "shapes" of sounds. There are many good videos on YouTube.com that you can watch to learn how to pronounce the sounds of letters and sounds that you may be having difficulty with. Practice using a mirror to see that you are shaping your mouth and a recorder to hear that you are recreating the sounds correctly.

**Remember that even native English speakers must use these techniques and do these exercises to improve their ability to speak well.**

# DEVELOPMENT OF SPEECH

There are three parts to developing your speech - introduction, body and conclusion. There is no reason to get fancy in your speech. In fact, the simpler and more concise you can keep your speech the better. Stick to the basics.

Part 1: Decide What Your Purpose Is.

Make sure you take a moment to decide what your purpose is; otherwise you will not be able to communicate it effectively.

Part 2: State the Topic.

For speaking tasks that ask you to present your opinion or to describe something personal to you, use the following introductory phrases:

I believe     I think     I feel     My view is     My opinion is     My preference is

After each of these statements, you will need to mention the topic and whatever example you are going to use.

For speaking tasks that ask you to summarize someone else's opinion or to explain facts, the following introductions are appropriate:

| This person believes that | This person's view is that | The reading stated |
|---|---|---|
| This person holds that | This person's point is that | The reading presented |
| This person argues that | The lecture stated | The lecture offered |

After each statement, fill in what the topic or position is.

Part 3: State "What" and "Why".

For speaking tasks that ask your opinion, you will have to state why you believe something.

For speaking tasks that require you to summarize facts or someone else's position, you will have to say what their reasons are.

Use the following words to indicate what and why:

because          the reason          due to          for          therefore

The speaking tasks on the TOEFL usually require you to do one of the following:

- Present your opinion on an issue (similar to the Writing Task)
- Explain facts presented in a lecture or reading.
- Summarize someone else's opinion.
- Describe something of importance to you.

Let's get started.

# BASIC PRINCIPLES

You do *not* have to sound like a native speaker of English to score well on the TOEFL iBT. It is perfectly acceptable to speak with an accent and make some mistakes in grammar and word use. What ultimately matters is how **understandable** your speech is. Structuring your words and timing your responses helps a lot.

Simply be aware of the following:

- How you sound. When speaking, you must try to avoid unnecessary pauses and speak at an even pace.
- What you say. Good responses have a clear flow of ideas and use appropriate transitions to link topics.
- Your command of English grammar and vocabulary. A top-scoring response uses a variety of words and contains some complex sentence structures.

The following are these principles in more detail.

## Basic Principle #1: How You Sound

Keep in mind that you don't have to sound like a native English speaker to give a high scoring response. However, you must speak confidently and clearly, with few long pauses and extra words interjected such as "uh" and "um".

The three biggest problems to avoid are:

- Pausing often and breaking up the flow of your speech with unnecessary words such as "um" and "uh".
- Delivering your speech in a mechanical "robot" voice, as if you were reading the response from a page.
- Calling the man in the passage "she" and/or calling the woman in the passage "he".

**The best way to avoid these problems is to think before you speak. Each task has a structure that must be followed to score well. Get to know these structures and practice them.**

Here are some tips to help overcome these common problems:

## PAUSES

One reason that a speaker may have many pauses in his or her response is a lack of confidence when speaking. RELAX. Remember that you are starting out with a score of 4 and all you need to do is answer the questions based on the type of task you are responding to clearly and directly.

Another reason that a speaker may have pauses in his or her response is that they are trying to translate from their native language into English as he or she speaks. The only way to solve this problem is with more practice speaking only in English. There is no quick and easy cure for not knowing the language. You must practice regularly.

Finally, the most common reason a speaker pauses while speaking is that they are "thinking while he or she is speaking". To avoid this problem you must practice taking notes of what you intend to speak about. Then, when speaking, keep your eyes on your notes and make sentences from what you have on the paper in front of you. In other words, use your notes and formulate simple sentences.

Remember to "think and then speak".

SPEAKING TIP: It is far easier to control your speech and grammar when making short sentences. So, in order to speak as a native English speaker, practice making short sentences and joining them together with connection words and phrases such as "but, and, or". Compound sentences are nothing more than two or more short sentences joined by a conjunction.

## ROBOT VOICE

Speakers often speak in a mechanical, choppy or "robot" voice because they are reading directly from their notes. One way to avoid this is to only write down the key words and phrases that you will speak about. However, the best way to avoid sounding mechanical is to practice your speaking. Get to know the tasks and listen to examples of proper responses. Practice the tasks using a variety of topics. The more you practice, the more natural you will sound.

<u>"HE/SHE"</u>

One of the most common problems speakers have is calling the man in the passage "she" and/or calling the woman in the passage "he". Although a simple and common error, this can seriously cost the speaker points. One way to avoid this is to keep track of your notes by who says what.

i.e: M – Hi, Gloria.

W – Hi, Alfred.

M – Have you seen the notice in the cafeteria?

W – No, what does it say?

Also, at the top of your notes write M = the man, he, him, his; and W = the woman, she, her, hers.  Refer to these notes when speaking and make a conscious effort to avoid making the gender mistake.

## Basic Principle #2: What You Say

Your speech should be clear and your sentences should be well connected. Use transition words that relate the parts of your speech together. Use words and phrases that will either link your idea to the main topic or to the previous sentence. Use the structures in the Reading and Listening sections as a guide.

i.e:    One reason         I believe         Also         For example   Furthermore

## Basic Principle #3: Command of English Grammar' and Vocabulary

You must have a basic mastery of grammar and vocabulary to score well on the TOEFL iBT. This class is not intended to teach you grammar or vocabulary. However, some basic grammatical structures and vocabulary words are provided in the Grammar Help section.

NOTE: The TOEFL Master strongly suggests that you spend the time you need in the Grammar Help section. Knowing the rules will allow you to construct sentences with greater ease and increase your confidence. Even if you are advanced in grammar and vocabulary do not try to be fancy to impress the judges. The rubric is simple and straightforward and you should keep that in mind.

## PREPARE FOR YOUR SPEECH

Follow these steps to a successful score on the Speaking Section:

## Part 1: Decide What Your Purpose Is.

You must begin your speech with an introduction and a statement of purpose. Simply introduce your subject or topic and state the main purpose of your speech. Take a moment to decide what your purpose is. Otherwise you will not be able to communicate the purpose effectively.

## Part 2: Answer the Prompt One Section at a Time.

Most prompts have several parts. They are actually several different questions in one. Answer them on part at a time.

> i.e. What was the problem the two students were discussing? Describe the problem, and state which solution is the best one. Give reasons and details to support your opinion.

Break this question into three parts and answer each one individually.

1. What was the problem?
2. Describe the problem.
3. Which one do you think is best?
4. What reason do you have for your choice?

## Part 3: Use Examples, Reasons and Details

All Speaking tasks require that you support your answers using examples or reasons and details. Be sure that you state examples or reasons and details accurately in the order they were presented in the reading and listening sections. Many people who speak English fluently fail this section simply because they do not fully answer the question. Be sure to provide all the information the task requires of you.

## Part 4: State "What" or "Why"

For speaking tasks that ask your opinion, you will have to state why you believe something. For speaking tasks that require you to summarize facts or someone else's opinion, you'll have to say what his or her reasons are.

Spoken responses on the TOEFL are only 45 - 60 seconds, so most of your time will be used presenting details or examples. Therefore, your introduction should be brief and to the point.

THAT IS THE KEY! Keep your speech brief and to the point.

## SPEAKING SECTION DIRECTIONS

The Speaking Section measures your ability to speak in English about a variety of topics. There are six questions in this section. Record your response to each question and email it to your tutor.

Questions 1 and 2 are independent speaking tasks in which you will speak about familiar topics. Your responses will be scored on your ability to speak clearly and coherently about the topics.

Questions 3 and 4 are integrated tasks in which you will read a passage, listen to a conversation or lecture, and then speak in response to a question about what you have read and heard. You will need to combine relevant information from the two sources to answer the question completely. Your responses will be scored on your ability to speak clearly and coherently and on your ability to accurately convey the information about what you have read and heard.

Questions 5 and 6 are integrated tasks in which you will listen to part of a conversation or lecture, and then speak in response to a question about what you have heard. Your responses will be scored on your ability to speak clearly and coherently and on your ability to accurately convey information about what you heard.

You will hear each conversation and lecture only one time. You may take notes while you listen. You may use your notes to help you answer the questions.

# QUESTION TYPES

There are six questions types in the Speaking Section of the TOEFL iBT. There are NO experimental sections in the Speaking Section and the question types always come in the same order. You must answer each question as it appears. Knowing the order will help you to prepare for taking notes and for structuring your responses.

**NOTE: The first two tasks require you to respond directly to a specific question using your own experiences.**

The main goal when answering each of these two question types is to answer each as concisely as you can while providing relevant reasons, examples, and details from your personal experiences or knowledge.

You will have 15 seconds to prepare your response and 45 seconds to respond to each question.

## Question Type 1 – Personal Preference

The first type of task on the Speaking Section of the TOEFL iBT asks you to speak of something that may be familiar to you. You may be asked to describe something you would like to do, a place that you prefer to go, something that is a favorite of yours, something you may want to see or experience, etc. Regardless of the exact question, you must choose the subject that you will speak about and use details and examples in your response to support your topic.

You will have 15 seconds to prepare and 45 seconds to respond to this question type.

For example:

**TASK: "Name your favorite food and explain why it is your favorite. Give reasons and details to support your response."**

In order to answer this question effectively **you must take notes** of your main ideas. Simply write

> Notes: Topic - Pizza
>
>> Reason - Nutritious
>>
>> Detail - Different vegetables/meats
>>
>> Reason - Cheese
>>
>> Detail - Love cheese
>>
>> Reason - Easy to make
>>
>> Detail - less than 30 min. to cook

From these notes you will make sentences, linking them together with connection words and phrases.

Sample HIGH LEVEL response:

> *"One of my favorite foods is pizza. I really like pizza because it is nutritious. I can make pizza with a large variety of vegetables and meats. Also, another reason that pizza is my favorite food is that it is covered in cheese and I just love cheese. Besides that, pizza is easy to make. I can usually make a pizza or get one made in less than thirty minutes."*

To make the task easier, break the questions into sections and answer each section individually. In other words, give each sentence as if you are answering a separate question.

Using the previous example:

**TASK: "Name your favorite food and explain why it is your favorite. Give reasons and details to support your response."**

First part of the question: Name your favorite food.

Sample response of favorite food: *"One of my favorite foods is pizza."*

Next respond to the second and third parts of the question: Explain why it is your favorite. Give reasons and details to support your response.

| | |
|---|---|
| Reason 1: | "I really like pizza because it is nutritious." |
| Detail: | "For one thing, I can make pizza with a large variety of vegetables and meats." |
| Reason 2: | "Also, another reason that pizza is my favorite food is that it is covered in cheese" |
| Detail: | "and I just love cheese." |
| Reason 3: | "Besides that, pizza is easy to make." |
| Detail: | "I can usually make a pizza or get one made in less than thirty minutes." |

As you can see, this response does not seem highly complex or sophisticated, but this response meets all of the criteria for the task and, if spoken correctly, it is a high scoring response. Besides, it is much more difficult to think when you are taking the test, so be sure to practice taking notes and speaking. Also, you may not be able to think of or have time to think of more than two reasons and details in fifteen seconds. That's o.kay. Just say what you are sure of and then be silent while the clock runs out.

**Remember: Don't try to sound too brainy. Just answer the question.**

Answering in this way makes it easier to structure your thoughts into manageable sentences, use connection words and phrases and reduces long pauses while thinking of how to express your thoughts.

If you do pause, do so between sentences and not during them. Pauses between sentences are less noticeable unless they are unnecessarily long.

## Question Type 2 – Choose an Option

The second type of task on the TOEFL iBT Speaking section will either give you two options to choose from or will ask whether you agree or disagree with a certain statement.

You will have 15 seconds to prepare and 45 seconds to respond to this question type.

For example:

"Some people believe that university students should be required to attend classes. Others believe that going to classes should be optional for students. Which point of view do you agree with? Use specific reasons and details to explain your answer."

Or:

"Do you agree or disagree with the following statement? Playing games teaches us about life. Use specific reasons and examples to support your answer."

Just as in Question Type 1, to answer this question effectively, you must take notes that center on your main ideas. Also, remember to break the questions into sections and answer each section individually.

**TASK: "Some people believe that university students should be required to attend classes. Others believe that going to classes should be optional for students. Which point of view do you agree with? Use specific reasons and details to explain your answer."**

Sample of a HIGH LEVEL response:

*"I believe students should be required to attend classes. One reason I believe it is better to attend classes is that students can hear the questions asked by other students. The answers to these questions can help a student understand the subject better. Another reason attending classes is better is that the professor often speaks about information that is not in the text books. Exams might have questions about information the professor spoke of only in class. And finally, a professor may give a surprise quiz and if a student isn't in class, they will not get credit for that quiz. This could lower the students overall grade for that class."*

This response answers the question directly in the first sentence and is followed by related reasons and details. It uses proper connection words and phrases to connect ideas, has different sentence structures and facilitates the use of proper grammar and vocabulary.

When spoken correctly, this response should last 30 – 45 seconds.

**TASK: "Do you agree or disagree with the following statement? Playing games teaches us about life. Use specific reasons and examples to support your answer."**

Sample of a HIGH LEVEL response:

*"Nothing teaches better than real life. However, I agree that playing games teaches us about life. Who hasn't played at being an adult when they were a child? When we are children, we watch the adults around us and try to copy what they are doing. This is one way of learning. Also, there are many video games designed to teach us about life such as the "The Sim's" games. These games can teach us how to manage a family, a home, a city or even how to build a theme park. Playing games is a good way to learn because a person can make mistakes without costing them a fortune or hurting anyone for real."*

This response answers the question directly in the first sentence and is followed by related reasons and details. It uses proper connection words and phrases to connect ideas, has different sentence structures and facilitates the use of proper grammar and vocabulary.

Follow the same basic structure and procedures used for answering Question Type 1 when formulating your response to these questions.

When spoken correctly, this response should last 30 – 45 seconds.

## THE CHALLENGE

One of the most difficult tasks is to think of a proper response in only fifteen seconds. The only way to make this easier is to practice, practice, and practice. Be sure to take notes of your preference, reasons and details/examples. Write down only your "key words" to each part of your response.

Although it is advisable that you not speak in a pre-determined format (template), having a particular structure to follow may help you to respond with more accuracy and confidence and makes your response easy for graders to understand. There is a "structure" that graders are listening for that, when used, will help you to achieve a higher score. Follow the basic structure described in this tutorial for a higher Speaking score.

Also, you should pace your responses and speak in clear, concise sentences using connection words and phrases to connect your ideas. Graders are listening for these connection words and phrases.

i.e. – For example   One reason   Furthermore   Because   Also   Another reason   Finally

Practice making complete, concise grammatically correct sentences and use vocabulary that you know to be appropriate.

Remember to break the questions into sections and answer each section individually. In other words, give each sentence as if you are answering a different question.

If you do pause, do so between sentences and not during them. Pauses between sentences are less noticeable unless they are unnecessarily long. Remember to "think and then speak".

Practice making complete, concise grammatically correct sentences and use vocabulary that you know to be appropriate.

Your responses for these tasks should be between 30 to 45 seconds.

Finally, there is no official penalty for speaking less than or going over the time given for the tasks, however, you should practice completing your response in the forty-five seconds given for each task.

NOTE: Be sure to write down your ideas and read from what you've written. Often when a speaker looks up at others around them or at the computer screen, they lose focus and begin to pause and fill the empty spaces with "uh" or "um" which lowers their score. Keep your eyes on your notes as you speak.

# **The next two tasks**

# **require you to read a passage and then listen to a related listening passage.**

The main goal when answering each of these two question types is to answer each question as concisely as you can by providing the details from the passages accurately in the order they appear in the passages.

You will have 30 seconds to prepare and 60 seconds to respond to each question.

## Question Type 3 – Summarize an Opinion

The third type of task on the Speaking Section of the TOEFL iBT requires you to take 45 seconds to read a brief announcement, and then listen to two students, a man and a woman, discuss the announcement and give their opinions about it. Your task is to take notes on the main topic of the announcement, the opinions of the two students, and their tone and attitudes. Following that you will respond to the question by using your notes.

The announcement will be a very short passage about something that has happened on campus that may affect the students. Following the announcement the two students will discuss the topic in twelve to fifteen exchanges. An exchange is where one student speaks and the other responds.

You will first hear a greeting between the two students. This is irrelevant and you need not take notes on this exchange. Following the greeting one student will ask the other if they had seen the announcement. Take notes on who gave their opinion first, why they have that opinion and of their tone or attitude toward the announcement. Are they excited, angry, confused or happy? Do they agree or disagree with the announcement? Why?

You will have 30 seconds to prepare and 60 seconds to respond to this question type.

For example:

### Notice of Change of Cafeteria Hours

Due to the high volume of freshmen this semester, the hours of operation for the campus cafeteria must be changed to accommodate the extra students. The cafeteria will now be open from 11:00 AM to 1:30 PM to only freshmen students. The cafeteria will be open from 1:30 P.M. to 4:30 P.M. for all other students. Students must show their student I.D. to be admitted to the cafeteria between the hours of 11:00 A.M. and 1:30 P.M. Again, this change is due to the high volume of freshmen this semester. Change in cafeteria hours will remain in effect until future notice.

**"Now listen to two students as they discuss the announcement."**

> **M:** Did you see the notice on the cafeteria doors?
>
> W: Yes… and it's going to be a problem for me.
>
> **M:** Really, how?
>
> W: Well, I have morning and afternoon classes. I usually take my lunch at 11:30 before my afternoon classes. My last class is over at 5:00. Now I won't have time to eat during the day.
>
> **M:** I see… maybe you could brown bag it. You know… carry your lunch with you to eat between classes?

W:   I suppose I could. But, I have physics and astronomy in the afternoons. I really like to have a hot, nutritious lunch before my afternoon classes to make sure my brain is really functioning well. Taking a cold sandwich and maybe a piece of fruit just doesn't sound like it will be enough.

M:   You're probably right. Hey! There's a small restaurant just off school campus. Maybe you could eat your lunch there each day?

W:   You mean the one on the corner with the cow out front? I've eaten dinner there and the food is pretty good, but kind of expensive for my budget. Not only is the cafeteria lunch hot, nutritious and convenient, it's pretty cheap. I don't think I can afford to eat my lunch at a restaurant every day.

M:   I see what you mean. I couldn't afford it either now that I think about it. So, what will you do?

W:   I don't know… maybe a combination of both? Just 'til the policy changes.

**TASK: "The woman has a problem with the new campus cafeteria hours. State the problem and explain what she intends to do about it."**

Sample of a HIGH LEVEL response:

*"The woman's problem is that she will not be able to have her lunch in the campus cafeteria like she usually does. She said that she needs to have lunch then because she has classes during the rest of the day. The man suggested two options. The woman could "brown bag" her lunch, meaning that she could carry her lunch in a bag during the day and eat it when she has the time. Or, she could eat at a restaurant close to the school campus. The woman was not happy with either option because she likes a hot lunch and doesn't have the money to eat at a restaurant every day, but she finally said that she may have to do a combination of both until the policy changes."*

As you can see by this response, the first sentence answers the question directly. The following sentences fill in the details from the conversation and the last sentence completes the response by addressing the second part of the question directly. Be sure to answer the question completely.

This response, when spoken correctly will last 45 – 60 seconds.

In the previous response, the question asked only that you relate the woman's problem and to state what she intends to do about it. However, there are other passages that give both the man's and the woman's opinion equally.

For example:

### Announcement of Course Schedule Change

Many students are already aware that a change is taking place in the Literature Department. Professor Spangler is retiring at the end of this semester and the university will sorely miss him. In the professor's absence, the university has had to make some adjustments to the schedule for the Early American Literature course. Beginning next semester, the evening class will be moved to the mornings and will be taught by Professor Biggs. The university wishes to express its gratitude to Professor Spangler for his many years of service and apologize to students for any inconvenience this change may have caused.

Now listen to two students as they discuss the announcement.

**W:** Have you heard that Professor Spangler is retiring?

M: Yes, and I'm not too happy about it.

**W:** You're not happy about it? Why?

M:     I was looking forward to being in his class next semester. I've heard that he really knows his subject and is an excellent professor. Now I will have to settle for a professor I've never heard of.

W:     I will be taking that same course next semester too. But, I'm sure the new professor will be a good one. I mean, the university wouldn't hire a professor who doesn't know their subject, would they?

M:     I don't know. I guess you're right about that.  It's just that I was looking forward to hearing Professor Spangler tell his stories that other students have told me about.

W:     I understand your disappointment, but try to keep a good attitude. Hopefully this professor will be just as animated.

M:     I certainly hope so.


**TASK: "The students discuss a change for an upcoming course. Describe the change and describe how each student feels about it and what they hope will happen. Use reasons and details to support your response."**

Sample of a HIGH LEVEL response:

*"The two students are talking about the retirement of an Early American Literature professor. The man is disappointed because he had heard from other students that Professor Spangler was a really good teacher. He was looking forward to hearing the professor's stories in class and now he will have to have someone different who may not teach the same way. The woman is not concerned about the change. She thinks that the university wouldn't hire a professor who doesn't know their subject. In the end, the two students hope the new professor will be a good one."*

As you can see by this response, the first sentence answers the question directly. The following sentences fill in the details from the conversation and the last sentence completes the response by addressing the second part of the question directly.

Be sure to answer the question completely.

This response, when spoken correctly will last 45 – 60 seconds.

Be sure to use your notes to create your response, relating the information accurately and in the order that it appeared in the passage.

## Question Type 4 – Summarize/Contrast Question

The fourth type of task on the Speaking Section of the TOEFL iBT requires you to take 45 seconds to read part of an academic lecture and then listen to part of a lecture on a related topic. Both the reading and the lecture will present certain main points and related details. You must take notes of the main topic and major points including any related details of both passages. Your task is to state the main topic and the relationship of both passages in an introductory statement, and then state how the two passages relate to the topic. Include specific points and details in your response in the order they appeared in the two passages.

While listening, note whether the professor agrees or opposes the reading section. Be sure to state this relationship in your response.

You will have 30 seconds to prepare your response and 60 seconds to respond to each passage.

For example:

**"Read the following passage about Shakespeare"** (excerpted from about.com)

Here's a startling statistic! New research by the RSC and British Council has revealed that approximately 50 percent of all schoolchildren in the world study Shakespeare each year ... Wow! Let's just take a moment to let that sink in. That's more than 64 million kids each year. A staggering 65 percent of the World's countries have Shakespeare as a named author in their curriculum. What's great about this statistic is the reason why they study Shakespeare. Half of the survey's respondents believe that Shakespeare should be taught because it is relevant to the issues that face young people today. Their contemporary issues and dilemmas are reflected in the plays.

**"Now listen to a professor lecture about the same topic."**

"Recently, I asked a very diversified class what Shakespeare's best play was and who was their favorite character. With 38 plays to choose from, I knew from the outset that this was a difficult question, but I was surprised by the responses nonetheless. Regardless of age, race, creed, religion or color, Shakespeare's plays seem to relate to the human character in such a way that everyone can put themselves into at least one of his characters. Although many students called out the obvious, *Romeo and Juliet,* their favorite character and the *reasons* that character was their favorite, were very different. Where I thought most would relate to either Romeo or Juliet, some of my students put themselves in the place of friends or family members. Another play, *Much Ado About Nothing,* was another that was stated as not being a favorite but one of the best. While discussing this play, it was clear that all of the students, no matter their background, found the issues discussed in the play relevant to their current experiences."

**TASK: "The professor describes a response to a question given in a class on Classic Literature. Explain how the response to this question relates to the reading on the topic."**

Sample of a HIGH LEVEL response:

*"Both passages are about how students can relate to the plays of Shakespeare. The reading passage states that a study done by RSC and British Council found a large percentage of schools worldwide teach Shakespeare's plays to their students. The reading also states that half of those people who responded to the study believe Shakespeare should be taught in schools because young people can relate to them. The listening supports the reading as the professor says that, in her class when students were asked what play they liked most and what character they identified with, regardless of the students' background, they could relate to some part of the different plays or their characters. Both passages indicate that the plays of Shakespeare represent universal issues and experiences of students."*

As you can see by this response, the first sentence answers the question directly and states the relationship between the two passages. The following two sentences express the details from the reading. The next sentence restates the relationship between the two passages and goes into the details from the listening passage. The last sentence completes the response by addressing the second part of the question directly.

Be sure to answer the question completely.

This response, when spoken correctly will last 45 – 60 seconds.

Questions of this type can also present passages that are opposed. Be sure to note the relationship of the two in your response.

Be sure to use your notes to create your response, relating the information accurately and in the order that it appeared in the passage.

The next two tasks require you to listen to a conversation between two students or a professor giving a lecture and then summarize what you have heard.

The main goal when answering each of these two question types is to answer each as concisely as you can while providing the details from the passages accurately in the order they appear in the passages.

You will have 30 seconds to prepare and 60 seconds to respond to each question type.

## Question Type 5 – Summarize/Preference Question

The fifth type of task on the Speaking Section of the TOEFL iBT requires you to listen to two students, a man and a woman, discuss a problem that one of them has and the two suggestions that are made by the other student, or discuss an assignment that both must complete and the two ways each student has of completing the assignment. Your task is to state the problem or the assignment (depending on the passage), the two possible solutions or the two different ways of handling the assignment, and then state which option you believe is best and why. Take notes on the main points of the passage. Note what the problem or assignment is. Also, note what the two options or two different ways of completing the assignment are. Listen to the opinions of the two students and note their tone and attitudes while taking notes. Respond to the question using your notes.

In the case of the problem/solution question, make sure to state first what the problem is. Be sure to identify if the problem is the man's or the woman's problem. Next, state what the two possible solutions are and who is giving the suggestions. Finally, state which of the solutions is best and explain why it is so according to the passage based on your notes, as indicated by reason, attitude or tone of the person offering the solutions.

For example:

W: Hi, Jeremy. How are you?

M: Fine… I guess. I'm facing a big problem though. It's the end of the semester and I have an assignment due Professor Dunley's class on Modern Architecture due next week. At the same time, I have to finish a report on the "psychology of marketing". I just don't have time to do them both. I don't know what to do, but if I don't get them both turned in on time, I won't have enough credits to graduate.

W: Oh, no! Have you spoken to your professors about it? Maybe one of them will give you a short extension?

M: I haven't yet. But, the other problem is that I have a job that takes my time too. I really need the money and can't afford to take time off.

W: I see…. You should still ask both of your professors if either of them could give a slight extension. Surely neither of them wants you to have to repeat the course?

M: I guess you're right. It is still going to be a whole lot of work though, and I'm not sure that I can finish it while working my job.

W: One thing's for sure. It's a lot of work either way, but if you don't ask for an extension, you won't get one. Then you'll really have troubles. It's better to ask now while there is still time.

M: I'm still afraid that, even with the extension, I won't be able to complete both assignments.

W: Well… the other thing you could do is to talk to your boss and take time off of work to finish your assignments. I understand that you need the money, but having to repeat a semester will definitely cost you more. Whatever you decide, you had better do it soon. Good luck.

M: Thanks. It looks like I've got a tough choice to make.


**TASK "Describe the man's dilemma and the suggestions the woman makes about how to manage it. What do you think the man should do, and why?"**


Sample of a HIGH LEVEL response:

*"It's the end of the semester and the man has two assignments due for two different classes, but he doesn't have enough time to finish them because he also works a job. The man is afraid that he won't be able to complete his assignments and won't graduate. The woman makes two suggestions. First, the man can ask his professor's for a short extension to complete his work. And second, the man can take time off from his job to get his assignments done on time. The man has a difficult decision to make because he said that he really needs the money from his job, so taking time off would be a problem for him. On the other hand, if he fails his courses, he will have to pay to take them again to graduate. I think the man should take off time from his work. Although he really needs the money, his school work must come first. If he fails his courses, he will have to pay a lot more than he is losing from taking time off from his job just to complete his two assignments."*

As you can see, the first two statements address the question directly by describing the man's problem. Next, the speaker briefly describes the two suggestions. Finally, the speaker states the solution that seems best based on the information provided by the speakers in the passage. That's the key. Use the information and tone of the speakers to determine which suggestion is best and why it is so.


This response, when spoken correctly, will last 45 – 60 seconds.

In the case of assignment question, state what the assignment is first. Then state what the two different ways of handling the assignment are. Be sure to state whether it was the man's or the woman's way of doing the assignment. Finally, state which of the ways of doing the assignment is best and why it is so according to the passage based on your notes, as indicated by reason, attitude or tone of the two students' conversation.

For example:

**M:** Hi, Kathy. Are you ready for the psych exam tomorrow in Professor Thompson's class?

W: Hey, Tommy. I think so. I really like that class. I find it so interesting

**M:** Me too. But it's a complicated class. I was wondering if we could compare notes?

W: I haven't been taking notes in class. I really understand what the professor is talking about, so I didn't think taking notes was necessary. Do you really think I should have?

**M:** Yes, I do. I can't tell you what to do, but taking notes is a part of getting good grades.

W: I didn't have to take notes in high school and I got good grades in my classes there.

**M:** Right. Well… you're in university now. Not only should you take notes, you might think about joining a study group. I belong to a several study groups. We meet to compare notes from each class and make sure that we aren't missing or misinterpreting something the professor said.

W: Maybe you're right. I just hate writing in class though. I seem to miss a lot of the lecture when I do.

**M:** That's the reason you need to join a study group. We each have "holes" in our notes and we meet to compare notes to fill in those gaps. It really helps to understand everything that is taught in class.

W: Maybe... I'll think about it.

**The students discuss how to prepare for an upcoming exam. Describe the two ways and state which one you think is better and why.**

Sample of a HIGH LEVEL response:

*"The two students have a psych exam the following day and the man asks the woman if they can compare notes. Both students find the class interesting, but the man says that the class is complicated and that he needs to take notes to understand what the professor is talking about. The woman says that she doesn't take notes in the class because she didn't take notes in high school and still got good grades. The man says that, not only should the woman take notes, but she should join a study group to compare notes. The woman says that she'll think about it. I think the man's way is better. Student's should take notes in their classes and also join a study group to compare their notes to be sure they have the right information. That way they will get good grades."*

This response is a good summary of the conversation offering some details from the talk. The conclusion is based on the information and tone of the speakers in the passage. That's the key. Use the tone and information of the speakers to determine the best solution.

This response, when spoken correctly will last 45 – 60 seconds.

## Question Type 6 – Summarize a Lecture Question

The fifth type of task on the Speaking Section of the TOEFL iBT requires you to listen to part of a lecture given by a professor that explains a term or concept and gives specific examples and details to explain the topic. This lecture will last 90 – 120 seconds long. Your task is to summarize the main points of either part of or the entire lecture using your notes using connection words and phrases. You must demonstrate that you understand the main ideas and relationships presented in the lecture.

You will have 20 seconds to prepare and 60 seconds to respond to this question type.

For example:

**"Listen to a lecture given in a music theory class."** (Excerpted from Wikipedia)

"Psychedelic rock is a style of rock music that is inspired or influenced by psychedelic culture and attempts to replicate and enhance the mind-altering experiences of psychedelic drugs. It emerged during the mid 1960s among folk rock and blues rock bands in United States and the United Kingdom. It often used new recording techniques and effects and drew on non-Western sources such the ragas and drones of Indian music. Psychedelic rock bridged the transition from early blues- and folk music-based rock to progressive rock, glam rock, hard rock, and as a result, influenced the development of sub-genres such as heavy metal.

By the end of the 1960's decade, psychedelic rock was in retreat. LSD had been made illegal in the US and UK in 1966. At the end of the year, the Altamont Free Concert in California, headlined by The Rolling Stones, became notorious for the fatal stabbing of black teenager Meredith Hunter by Hells Angel security guards. Brian Wilson of the Beach Boys, Brian Jones of the Rolling Stones, Peter Green of Fleetwood Mac and Syd Barrett of Pink Floyd were early "acid casualties", helping to shift the focus of the respective bands of which they had been leading figures. Some bands like the Jimi Hendrix Experience and Cream broke up. Jimi Hendrix died in London in September 1970, shortly after recording Band of Gypsies, Janis Joplin died of a heroin overdose in October 1970 and they were closely followed by Jim Morrison of the Doors, who died in Paris in July 1971. Many surviving acts moved away from psychedelia into either more back-to-basics "roots rock", traditional-based, pastoral or whimsical folk, the wider experimentation of progressive rock, or to riff-laden heavy rock."

**TASK: "Using points and examples from the talk, explain why psychedelic rock was virtually abandoned by music artists."**

Sample of a HIGH LEVEL response:

*"According to the professor, psychedelic rock was only really popular for the last half of the 1960's era. That kind of music was embraced by a culture that used psychedelic drugs and who tried to create music that would enhance the effects of those drug experiences. The professor said that in 1966 a young black girl was killed at a concert featuring this type of music, and that psychedelic rock lost most of its popularity between the late 1960's and early 70's when many of the performers died of drug overdose. These instances apparently led to the shift away from that type of style. At that time many bands switched to other forms of rock music."*

This response begins by addressing the main topic and giving a brief description of it followed by examples and details given in the lecture which fully answer the question.

This response, when spoken correctly will last 45 – 60 seconds.

FINAL NOTE: This task is designed to gauge a student's ability to understand and to respond to certain academic situations. It is a basic skills test. This is not an acceptance speech for a Grammy Award. No one, other than the graders of the test, will be reviewing your responses, so keep them direct and to the point using your notes and understanding of the passages to answer them.

Relax, follow your notes, follow the basic response structures and speak clearly.

Practice until you are comfortable responding to the separate tasks and you will do fine.

# TAKING RELEVANT NOTES

Refer back to the explanation of **Question #1** to see how to take notes regarding that particular question type.

For **Question #2** use the same structure and method of taking notes as question #1. Be sure to be as brief as possible and only write down the key words for each main idea. Use these key words to make your sentences.

For the last four questions keep in mind that your task is to state the information accurately and in the order it appears in the passage.

When taking notes for **Question #3**, follow the structure below for a high-level response. Make to take notes as you read and hear the conversation as there will not be enough time to do so between the conversations and time to answer. There will be a written announcement for you to read followed by a conversation. The conversation will always be between a man and a woman. So, make a list like the following:

**Announcement**: Write a brief description of announcement. Just one sentence that gives the general idea of what it is about.

Then write "M" and "W" in a column to take notes of these points:

**M**: Man's Opinion and statement of why he holds that opinion, or of how he feels about the announcement.

**W**: Woman's Opinion and statement of why she holds that opinion, or of how she feels about the announcement.

**Related Details**: Make notes of any details mentioned related to the announcement.

**NOTE**: Be sure to keep your notes clear and in the order the information is presented in the passage.

First, summarize the announcement. This is a brief sentence that states only the basic idea of what the reading passage was about. Then, begin taking notes of which speaker gives their opinion first. In other words, if the man gives his opinion first take notes of his opinion and relate them first in your response followed by the woman's response if asked to do so. Furthermore, take additional notes of any details related to the main topic of the announcement. There may not be any additional details, so do expect to hear them always.

When giving your response, be sure to answer the question appropriately. Begin with an introduction that states what the discussion was about.

**NOTE:** If the question asks only about the man's opinion, give only the man's opinion. If the question asks only for the woman's opinion, give only the woman's opinion. If the question asks for the opinion of both students, relate their opinions accurately in the order given in the passage.

**NOTE**: Remember that the pronouns used for the woman are either "she", "her," or "hers," and the pronouns used for the man are either "he," "him," or "his." Mixing them could cost you a point.

When taking notes for the different styles of **Question #4**, follow the structure below for a high-level response. There will be a written passage for you to read followed by a lecture related to the reading. There are two styles this question may come in:

## QUESTION #4 – INTEGRATED TASK TYPE #1
There are two types of so-called Integrated Task questions. In one type, the reading will state a main topic supported by two main points with related details, and the listening passage will have the same main topic and match the reading point for point. The reading often states some kind of definition of the topic or theory regarding the topic, while in the listening the professor states a real-life situation that depicts what actually happened. There may be as many as four main points but there are usually only two. The related points from the listening passage will either support or oppose the reading passage. Taking your notes using the structure illustrated below will help you to organize the information and to state your relationships accurately. When responding, make sure that you structure your response in the order the information comes in the READING section for this type of question. Be sure to mark whether the listening passage supports or opposes the reading passage.

**Supports — "Main Topic" — Opposed  (Circle one)**

| **Reading** | **Listening** |
|-------------|---------------|
| MP: | RMP 1: |
| Detail: | Detail: |
| MP: | RMP 2: |
| Detail: | Detail: |
| MP: | RMP 3: |
| Detail: | Detail: |
| MP: | RMP 4: |
| Detail: | Detail: |

**\* MP = Main Point / RMP = Related Main Point**

# STRUCTURE FOR THIS TYPE OF QUESTION #4

If your reading passage is in the form of a main topic followed by two related main points and their supporting details, begin your response by giving a brief summary of both the reading and listening passages that clearly states the relationship between the two. (Both related points will be either supportive or opposing.) Then, summarize the first main point from the reading passage, along with its related details and state how it relates to the corresponding main point in the listening passage. Repeat this structure for the second point from both passages. Be sure to state the relationships between the reading and listening sections for each main point. When complete, this response will have an introduction statement that summarizes the two passages and clearly states whether they are supportive or opposing followed by statements of both main points and details from each passage that clearly states their relationship.

# QUESTION #4 – INTEGRATED TASK TYPE #2

In the other type of Integrated Task, the reading may state a problem and a proposed solution, while in the listening the professor will talk about what actually happened when the proposal was put into practice. Using the structure illustrated below will enable you to state the details accurately in the order they appear in each passage.

### Supports – "Main Topic" – Opposes

| Reading | Listening |
|---|---|
| Problem: | Actual Outcome: |
| Discussion of | |
| Possible Solutions: | |
| Proposed Solution: | |

# STRUCTURE FOR THIS TYPE OF QUESTION

If your reading passage is in this form, begin your response with an introduction that summarizes both passages and states their relationship. Then, give a summary of the reading passage. Be sure to state all the details accurately and in the order they appear in the reading. Finally, end your response with a statement of the relationship between the reading and listening passage, and then state what was discussed in the listening passage accurately and in the order the information appeared.

**NOTE**: Regardless of which type you have on your TOEFL iBT, keep your response to just summarizing the main points and stating the relationship between the reading

The structure for **Question #5** is very direct. You will hear a conversation between a student and a campus official regarding a problem the student is having. Simply take notes of the problem, the two possible solutions, the tone of the of the person offering the solutions, and of the solution that the passage indicates is the "best" one. The tone of the official will often give away which solution they believe is best. Follow their lead in giving your response.

Take your notes in the structure below. Remember to not write in full sentences.
Problem:
Possible Solution #1:
Tone:
Detail:
Possible Solution #2:
Tone:
Detail:

**Question #6** requires you to listen to a lecture that is about 1 1/2 minutes in length and to take notes on the main points and related details. Be sure to right down the main topic, the main points the professor makes about the topic and the related details of each main point. The question will either you to use all or only part of your notes. If the question asks about the passage in general, simply begin at the top of your notes and use them to relate as much of the passage as possible accurately and in the order of your notes. If the question asks about a specific detail from the passage, state the main topic and then use only the notes you need to answer the question.

# TOEFL Speaking Section Progress Report

Student's Name: _____ Date: _____

Use this form to track your ability to answer certain question types.

Test # 1 2 3 4 5 6 (Circle One)

Question Type

Independent Tasks Number 1 ____ Number 2 ____

Integrated Tasks Number 3 ____ Number 4 ____

Number 5 ____ Number 6 ____


Rubric Summary:

Answer with Yes (Y) or No (N)

Did you speak in English _____

Did you answer the question _____

Did you speak clearly _____

Did you have any long pauses or extra words _____

Did you use relevant examples and details _____

Did you use accurate examples and details in the order presented (Q# 3–6 only ) _____

Did you use transition words and phrases _____

Did you have proper grammar and vocabulary _____

NOTES:_____

_____

_____

_____

_____

_____

# Part III - Resources

**Chapter 7: Basic Grammar**
**Chapter 8: Commonly Asked Questions**

## Chapter 7 – Basic Grammar

This section is not intended to fulfill all of your grammar needs, but rather simply to give a few pointers on how to construct sentences in the American-English style. Most students worry about all the advanced grammar, but it is with the little things that they make the most mistakes. For instance, simple conjugations, verb forms, and verb tenses challenge non-native speakers. This chapter will give helpful tips on basic and complex sentence structures that you can use to write effective essays.

There are three areas of grammar that most of my students have struggled with over the years the most:   VERBS, PREPOSITIONS, and TRANSITIONAL PHRASES.

First of all, in general, American English has the opposite structure of most languages in the world because American English is presented primarily in the active voice as compared to the passive voice structure.

To speak and write in the active voice, the structure is simple: Subject–Verb–Object.

Example of the active voice structure: "Johnny took his bicycle to school and locked it up outside."
Example of the passive voice structure: "The bicycle was taken to school and locked up by Johnny." Or, "Johnny's bicycle was taken to school and locked up by him."

Although these sentences may seem to present the same information, they are slightly different in meaning. First of all, the first sentence makes it clear that the bicycle belongs to Johnny, while the ownership of the bicycle in the second sentence is undetermined. Although the third sentence does clarify that the bicycle belongs to Johnny, it is still in the passive voice.

The graders for ETS prefer essays written in the active voice. Therefore, this section will help you to understand basic sentence structures that will enable you to speak and write in the active voice.

**Below is a table of the ten most common verb constructions in the active voice.**
Bare Infinitive – Form of verb without the verb "to" in front of it. i.e. – work, play, jump

Present participle – Form of verb with the "ing" ending. i.e. – working, playing, jumping

Past Participle – Form of verb with the "ed" ending. i.e. – worked, played, jumped

| <u>Verb Tenses</u> | <u>Auxiliaries</u> | <u>Verb Forms</u> |
|---|---|---|
| Simple Present | do/does | Bare Infinitive |
| Present Continuous | am/is/are | Present Participle |
| Present Perfect | have/has | Past Participle |
| Present Perfect Continuous | have/has been | Present Participle |
| Simple Past | did | Bare Infinitive |
| Past Continuous | was/were | Present Participle |
| Past Perfect | had | Past Participle |
| Past Perfect Continuous | had been | Present Participle |
| Simple Present of "to be" | am | Bare Infinitive |
| Simple Past of "to be" | was | Bare Infinitive |

## CONJUGATIONS

There are two basic verb types: the "to be" verb, and verbs other than the verb "to be."

## THE "TO BE" VERB

The simple present of the "to be" verb is conjugated in the active voice as follows:

| Without Contraction | With Contractions |
|---|---|
| I am | I'm |
| You are | You're |
| He is | He's |
| She is | She's |
| It is | It's |
| We are | We're |
| They are | They're |

**NOTICE** that the verb changes for "he, she, and it." They are considered third person singular. Regular verbs other than the verb "to be" are noted by one common feature. Following "he, she, and it" they use the ending "s."

## REGULAR VERBS OTHER THAN "TO BE"

The simple present of all other verbs are conjugated in the active voice as follows:

| | | |
|---|---|---|
| I work | I play | I sleep |
| You work | You play | You sleep |
| He works | He plays | He sleeps |
| She works | She plays | She sleeps |
| It works | It plays | It sleeps |
| We work | We work | We sleep |
| They work | They work | They sleep |

NOTICE that the singular form of the verb ends in "s".

Verbs other than "to be" form questions and negative statements using the auxiliary verb "do." These verbs are conjugated as listed below, using the regular verb "to work":

| Conjugation | Example Question | Example Negative Statement |
|---|---|---|
| I do work | Do I work? | I do not work. |
| You do work | Do you work? | You do not work. |
| He does work | Does he work? | He does not work. |
| She does work | Does she work? | She does not work. |
| It does work | Does it work? | It does not work. |
| We do work | Do we work? | We do not work. |
| They do work | Do they work? | They do not work. |

BASIC SENTENCE STRUCTURES

There are six basic sentence structures in the active voice. The different verb forms and tenses are given in the examples as follows (in this case, using the verb "to be"):

**Affirmative Statement**

I am ready.　　　You are ready.　　　He is ready.　　　She is ready.

It is ready.　　　We are ready.　　　They are ready.

**Question**

Am I ready?　　　Are you ready?　　Is he ready?　　　Is she ready?

Is it ready?　　　Are we ready?　　Are they ready?

**Negative Statement**

I am not ready.　　You are not ready?　　He is not ready?　　She is not ready?

It is not ready?　　We are not ready?　　They are not ready?

**Negative Question**

Am I not tired?　　Are you not ready?　　Is he not ready?　　Is she not ready?

Is it not ready?　　Are we not ready?　　Are they not ready?

**Negative Question with Contraction**

Am I not ready?      Aren't you ready?      Isn't he ready?      Isn't she ready?

Isn't it ready?      Aren't we ready?      Aren't they ready?


**Negative Question with Tag Question**

I am ready, am I not?

You are ready, aren't you?

He is ready, isn't he?

She is ready, isn't she?

It is ready, isn't it?

We are ready, aren't we?

They are ready, aren't they?


## COMMON GRAMMATICAL ERRORS

In my six-month grammar class, students are always trying to get my to help them with the most complicated parts of grammar. They think that learning the most complex parts of grammar will make them better speakers and writers. But the truth is that it is the basics in which people make the most mistakes: Things like subject/verb agreement, subject/pronoun agreement, pronoun ambiguity, using proper prepositions, joining sentences (clauses), and using the proper punctuation. These common errors can destroy a TOEFL score, so let's get started on correcting them.


## SUBJECT/VERB AGREEMENT

The first and most common problem is subject/verb agreement. The rule for this is simple: Singular with singular—plural with plural. In other words, if the subject is singular you must use the singular form of the verb. Conversely, if the subject is plural, you must use the plural form of the verb.

Incorrect: My friends was visiting me over the weekend.
Correct:   My friends were visiting me over the weekend.

It may help you to know the different singular and plural verbs.

| Singular (I) | Third Person Singular (he, she, it, who) | Plural (we, they, you) |
|---|---|---|
| am | is | are |
| do | does | do |
| did | did | did |
| was | was | were |
| have | has | have |

Some subjects seem plural because they are made up of many people, but also take a singular verb:

family
audience
The United States (or any other country)
group
jury
team
congregation

*Each of these subjects above usually use the verb **is**.

Many pronouns also must take a singular verb:

either
anyone
neither
no one
none
someone
each
everyone
one

*Each of these pronouns above always use the verb **is**.

A little known rule for verb agreement is with the use of the words "or" and "nor." This rule is also simple: When the subject following "or" or "nor" is singular, the verb is singular. When the subject following "or" or "nor" is plural, the verb is plural.

i.e. – Either one apple or two pears are needed to make the pie.
Either two apples or one pear is needed to make the pie.
Neither one apple nor two pears are needed to make the pie.
Neither two apples nor one pear is needed to make the pie.

Another rule for "or" and "nor" is their relationship to "neither" and "nor."

Either . . . or - neither . . . nor.

An easy way to remember this rule is by thinking that they go together like pairs of shoes and gloves. You wouldn't put a glove on one hand and a shoe on the other, would you?

So, sentences must read: neither . . . nor . . . **or** either . . . or . . . This is a simple rule, but is often confused.

Plural subjects often end in the letter "s," but subjects may also be made plural by using the word "and" to join them.

i.e. – Bob and Tom are my best friends.

In this sentence, "Bob and Tom" is considered a compound subject, which makes it plural.

Compound subjects **always** use a plural verb.

**NOTE:** When and is used in the NAME of something such as "peaches and cream", or "War and Peace", or "Jones, Smith, and Johnson" is it considered singular.

## PRONOUN AGREEMENT

The rule for pronoun agreement with their subjects is simple: singular with singular and plural with plural.

Incorrect: Everyone in the room believed their answer was the best one.

Incorrect: Everyone in the room believed their answers were the best ones.

Correct: Everyone in the room believed his or her answer was the best one.

## PRONOUN AMBIGUITY

Pronoun ambiguity occurs when it is unclear to which subject the pronoun is referring. This error is very common when speaking or writing in English. Therefore, when speaking or writing be sure to consider your audience. Keep in mind that people do not know what you are thinking, so be careful when discussing two subjects that are relating to each other.

Incorrect: After waiting three long days, the postman told the customer that he should be getting his mail.

Question: Who should be getting "his" mail—the postman or the customer? Who knows? The sentence is ambiguous.

Correct: After waiting three long days, the postman told the customer, "You should be receiving your mail."

## PASSIVE VOICE

American English is the opposite of many languages in the world where people speak and write in the passive voice. When speaking and writing in English (especially on the TOEFL), it is best to present the information in the active voice.

The structure for the active voice is simple: Subject – Verb – Object.
**Answers the question, "Who or what is doing what?"**

Passive Voice: The TOEFL iBT was taken by him.

Active Voice: He took the TOEFL iBT.

Passive Voice: By attending a university we become better prepared to live a successful life.

Active Voice: We become better prepared to live a successful life by attending a university.

## WORDINESS

Wordiness typically occurs when we try to explain more than is necessary using repetitive phrases unnecessarily.

Incorrect: While taking the test, I kept hearing people talking, which disturbed me while I was taking the test.
Correct: The people talking during the test disturbed me.

## PUNCTUATION AND CAPITALIZATION

The first word of a sentence always begins with a capital letter. Also, proper nouns such as names of people, businesses, and countries all begin with a capital letter.

Sentences usually end in one of three types of punctuation.
Period ( . ) – A general statement ends in a period.
Question Mark ( ? ) – A question ends in a question mark.
Exclamation Point ( ! ) – An emphatic statement ends in an exclamation mark.

NOTE: Remember that a sentence contains a subject, verb, and an object. Keep your sentences short, to the point, and in the active voice.

# Chapter 8 – Commonly Asked Questions

**Q:** **Do I have to take the TOEFL iBT to enter a university?**

**A:** Many universities do require that you meet a minimum score on the TOEFL iBT. There are other tests that you might be able to take to determine your level of English proficiency, however, the TOEFL iBT is the most widely accepted test being accepted by over 7,300 colleges and universities in 130 countries worldwide.

**Q:** **What score do I have to have to apply to a university?**

**A:** With over a million students a year taking the TOEFL iBT, the average score is 68. However, the average minimum score for applying to most universities is 80. Each university has its own requirement for a minimum TOEFL iBT score, so check with the university that you are wanting to attend. To find out what score you need to have, check the admissions area at the web site of the university you would like to attend.

**TIP:** The scores listed on the sites are the MINIMUM required to APPLY. Meeting these scores will NOT guarantee admission to a University. However, not meeting them may prevent admission. My advice is to do your best to score at least 5-10 points higher than the minimum score. Doing this may be more difficult, but your efforts will really pay off in a higher GPA. (Grade Point Average)

**Q:  How can I get a higher score on the TOEFL iBT?**

A:  PRACTICE, PRACTICE, PRACTICE!!!


TIP:  The average score on the TOEFL iBT is 68, but the average minimum score to enter many universities is 80. As a rule, for every point you want to score over 68, you must practice for two hours taking the test the correct way. To do this, follow all of the instructions in this course for test taking and visit the links provided to help with any grammar and vocabulary problems that you may be having.

REMEMBER: Minimum effort produces minimum return.

Maximum effort produces maximum return.


**Q:  Is the "TOEFL Master's Guide" affiliated with ETS?**

A:  NO! This TOEFL iBT is owned and copyrighted by PraxisGroup International Language AKADEMEIA, LLC, a private institute that is dedicated to teaching students who desire apply to universities in the United States or other English speaking countries how to achieve a higher score on the TOEFL iBT.

TOEFL iBT is a registered trademark of ETS (Educational Testing Services).


**Q:  Do you offer scored tests for the SPEAKING and WRITING sections?**

A:  YES!!! Email **william@pgila.org** and request a "Speaking Section Score". An online tutor will score all Speaking and Writing assignments for you.

**Q:** **Is the TOEFL iBT test automated or is there an actual grader who judges the Speaking Section Responses?**

**A:** Although sections of the TOEFL iBT are automated, such as the multiple choice answers for the Reading and Listening sections, you do have live graders who actually listen to and read your Speaking and Writing section responses.

**Q:** **Do you also offer an English grammar course online?**

**A:** Although we do give classroom English grammar courses, we do not offer them online at this time. However, you may wish to attends private courses that we give in Estero, Florida, USA. For more information, please contact us at william@pgila.org. See our website: www.pgila.org

**Q:** **How long are the TOEFL Master courses?**

**A:** Our private courses are 30 days in length.

**Q:** **How do I register for the TOEFL iBT?**

**A:** You can register easily at: http://ets.org/toefl/ibt/about
Follow this link and Click on the blue "Register Now" button on the left hand side of the screen. Have your ID card in hand to answer the questions correctly as any mistakes are very difficult to correct.

Also, have the names of three universities that you would like your scores sent to handy to fill in that section when you get to it.

Finally, follow the directions and have your (parents) credit card ready to pay for your test registration. Print the receipt once your registration is completed.

Q:     **What if I have questions regarding the TOEFL iBT test itself?**

A:     For questions regarding the TOEFL iBT test please go to:

http://ets.org/toefl/ibt/faq/


Q:     **How do I sign up for private courses?**

A:     Contact Dr. Gonzales-Hearn at drlizzie@pgila.org and ask to register for classes.


# Epilog:

In the end, it all comes down to this: the TOEFL test besides, speaking in English is all about you being understood and you understanding others. You don't have to speak perfectly for that. In fact, most native English speakers don't speak English perfectly at all, but we still do just fine, so don't worry about making little mistakes. Just think of your purpose and decide on your sentence structure first. In other words, are you making a statement or asking a question? Then, structure your sentence accordingly. There is one thing my students find out for sure: once you stop trying to be "perfect", speaking in English is a lot easier and a lot more fun.

Good luck with fulfilling your dreams, and please let me know how you are doing!!

Made in the USA
Las Vegas, NV
31 January 2025